# THE
# 52
# WEEK
# PROJECT

LAUREN KEENAN

# THE 52 WEEK PROJECT

### HOW I FIXED MY LIFE BY TRYING A NEW THING EVERY WEEK FOR A YEAR

ALLEN&UNWIN

SYDNEY · MELBOURNE · AUCKLAND · LONDON

First published in 2020

The quote on page 7 and 28 is widely attributed
to Dr Seuss, but can't be found in his work.

Allen & Unwin
Level 2, 10 College Hill, Freemans Bay
Auckland 1011, New Zealand
Phone: (64 9) 377 3800
Email: auckland@allenandunwin.com
Web: www.allenandunwin.co.nz

83 Alexander Street
Crows Nest NSW 2065, Australia
Phone: (61 2) 8425 0100

A catalogue record for this book is available from
the National Library of New Zealand.

ISBN 978 1 98854 750 3

Design by Megan van Staden
Set in Baskerville and Van Goth
Printed and bound in Australia by Griffin Press, part of Ovato

10 9 8 7 6 5 4 3 2

MIX
Paper from
responsible sources
FSC
www.fsc.org    FSC® C009448

The paper in this book is FSC® certified.
FSC® promotes environmentally responsible,
socially beneficial and economically viable
management of the world's forests.

This book is for all of the people who were
there for one of my new things:

Tane, Steph, Shirley, Terri, Bri, Emily, Ellen, Liv,
Alex, Patrick, Ben, Maria, Rachel H, Danny, Gaylene,
Stephen, Marilyn, Raema, Ray, Amotai, Lily, Kelly,
Bassie, Julia, Cathy, Kristen, Greg, George, Philippa,
Erin, Ngaire, Jessica, Rebecca, Sarah F, Phil, Ange,
Tracey, Katrina, Elizabeth, Lisette, Louis, Erika,
Lawry, Sarah C, Polly, Sarah B, Rachel W, Paul, Joe,
Miriama, Sarah J, Bonnie, Mae, Holly and Erina

'You'll never be bored when you try something new.
There's really no limit to what you can do.'
—Dr Seuss

Courtney Caile
Falmouth Bookseller
2022

# CONTENTS

# 1

## TWENTY-SEVEN REJECTIONS OF DOOM

✳ **New thing 1:** Doing a confidence course through the forest treetops

**THE WINTER BEFORE MY YEAR OF** new things, my script ran out.

The script, or variations on the script, will be familiar to many of you: go to school, get a job, meet a special someone, have children. Followed, for me, by the treadmill of juggling work and parenting, and the gnawing feeling of not succeeding at either. It's a script of to-do lists that seem dull and forgettable. But you can't *actually* forget the things on the list. If you do, your suit isn't dry-cleaned in time for that important meeting, your bills are paid late, and your child is the only one in their class without a banana on World Banana Day. It's a mental load that can leave you with constant low-level anxiety about having forgotten to do something important, but not being completely sure what that thing is, so just hoping it won't lead to burning your house down, getting fired or becoming a social pariah.

My own script was particularly unoriginal. School, university, first job. Then, in no particular order: exchanging of vows, house, children. Alan was two years older and ten centimetres taller. I had a boy and a girl exactly two years apart, and a house in the sort of neighbourhood where children play in the street. All I needed was the white picket fence. In a radical divergence from the script, Alan and I had opted for a practical wooden fence of the non-picket variety instead. Pickets are too hard to paint, we had been told.

I didn't consciously fall into line like a lemming as I lurched from chapter to chapter of the script, or make decisions because of external pressure. I wanted each and every chapter of my script. I was and continue to be grateful that I've been able to follow the script I have. There are many people who would dearly love to do the same, but cannot, for a myriad of reasons. Other people's scripts are less painfully middle class. I agree with Kieran Setiya, who wrote: 'I recognize the luxury of the midlife crisis, with a degree of guilt and shame.'[1] The rational part of my brain knew that I was lucky. Very lucky. Having my script run out is much luckier than having it hairpin in an unplanned direction via injury or illness. I hadn't been forced to live the 'Option B' Sheryl Sandberg describes in her book about coming to terms with her husband's death.[2] I had been lucky to have children, and to be in a position to buy a house. Things weren't so bad, not compared to the suffering of other people. I wasn't poor or sick or hungry. During that winter, knowing I was lucky but feeling shit nonetheless was yet another strand of the self-flagellation whip I used to beat myself with. My problems were very much the sort deserving of the label #firstworldproblems. In fact, they were #privilegedmiddleclassproblems.

And yet . . .

I had followed the script ever since I was a teenager, and it had run out of words.

There is a stereotypical script for men when they face this life stage, the 'classic' midlife crisis involving red convertibles, young secretaries and bad toupees. We've all seen the movies, read the books, and probably know a few real-life examples as well. It's different for women. According to pop culture, we can take one of two midlife-crisis journeys: be galvanised into reforming our dowdy post-children selves after the men in our lives embrace the 'classic' man script as described above, or take up yoga. Neither of these options worked for me. Alan hadn't consigned me to the first-wives club, and yoga didn't appeal to me—I'm as flexible as a plank of wood. Besides, who has time for soul searching when you get only a few weeks of annual leave a year, and most of that is consumed by school holidays? I couldn't have one of those sorts of mid-life crises. If I did, the ever-present mental load would eat me alive. I had children, a mortgage, a job—a life that wouldn't stand still while I 'found myself'. Any self-indulgent navel-gazing of the finding-oneself variety needed to happen within the margins of my daily routine. I didn't have *time* to change. I'd just keep bobbing downstream and hope that I didn't drown.

And then Alan and I separated. We were fine, we were strong. And then we weren't. It was as if we'd read a bit of click-bait entitled 'How to grow apart in ten easy steps' and followed it to the letter. There's no script for marriage breakdown, apart from the seek-revenge-by-becoming-super-hot trope. There's certainly no script when there isn't a victim/perpetrator dynamic: no one had an affair; no one was beaten; no one was emotionally abusive. Neither of us thought that yonder grass was greener, but we'd still managed to kill our own grass by failing to water it properly. It makes people uncomfortable when they can't immediately hook into a straightforward explanation of why two people with a house and children might not want to be together anymore. I found vague explanations about 'growing apart' made people especially uncomfortable. They trust that their own relationship is safe from affairs and abuse and being traded in for the pool boy. Growing apart, though? Now that's a scary thought. It's the one explanation that they know might one day apply to them if they're not careful.

It's stating the obvious, but breakups really are dire. I guess that's why people have been writing bad poetry about them for millennia. I wouldn't be surprised if those famous ancient cave drawings in France weren't actually depicting a breakup, albeit one involving mammoths. It didn't help that Alan and I separated in autumn, so I had a cold and miserable winter to process my new, hollow life. Isn't winter awful? I think so. I've never been a fan, not once the novelty of hot soup and mulled wine wears off. In winter, places with colder climates have 40 per cent more Google searches about depression than places with warmer climates.[3] I'm not surprised. That winter before the year of new things, it was me plugging 'Am I depressed?' into Google. It was a dreary winter without colour. Okay, I lie: I did have one thing that was colourful—a bright purple notebook I'd bought for the simple reason that I was sad and wanted to buy something to cheer me up. I bought a purple pen to match, a fat pen with thick ink that soaked through the pages in smudgy, purple glory. When I got home, I put the pen and notebook on my bed, and berated myself. What the hell did I need a purple notebook for? I then picked up the pen, opened the notebook, and wrote a list. It went:

**Things that made me feel bad today**
1. I wasted money on a notebook and pen
2. I hate purple
3. This pen sucks.

I then wrote other things that had made me feel bad: the thought that I was letting my children down; the fact that my friend hadn't replied to a message I'd sent; an argument with Alan about the extractor fan; eating too much cake. It was depressing and cathartic in equal measure. Then, on the next page, another list: *Things that brought me joy today*. I had to think about it, but there were more things than I'd expected: dancing with the children; a funny joke; a phone call from my mum. I liked the lists so much I wrote them every day for a month. It turned out to be the first rung of the ladder out of the cesspit, although that's not why I continued. I kept going because I had no one to talk to, and writing my thoughts in a notebook made me feel like they were real and worthy. It made me feel less like that tree that falls in the forest, far from human ears, where it may or may not have made a sound. I felt less alone, writing for my own future self. Sometimes the lists felt daft; of course I knew what made me happy and sad. Some of the things on the lists weren't rocket science—laughing made me happy, and loss made me sad. Quality time with people I love made me happy, and dropping my dry-cleaning in a puddle within half an hour of having collected it made me sad. And sometimes what had made me happy (eating that entire block of chocolate) also made me sad (feeling disgusting after eating aforementioned block of chocolate).

Yet, I persisted.

Some patterns emerged, things I hadn't quite realised before. One of the things that consistently made me feel the worst was when I had plans with other people that changed—a last-minute cancellation, or looking forward to doing something that didn't pan out as anticipated. I wasn't resilient enough to deal with rejection. My friends aren't assholes; when plans were shifted or cancelled it was always with good reason. It was me that had changed, with my poor, worn-down mental armour. Knowing I was being unreasonable and over-emotional made me feel even worse. I felt bad when people cancelled on me, then I felt bad that I felt bad, pulling out the self-flagellation whip and rubbing salt into my own wounds. I was also ashamed of how rotten I felt, telling people 'No worries!' and 'All good, catch you next time!' before going home to cry. Loneliness is a very difficult thing to admit, even to your innermost self.

So what made me happy? There were the little moments with the children: taking advantage of the very narrow window in which they find me funny by inventing a robot dance; reading to them; a rare evening when both went to bed without tears or yelling or requests for six hundred million glasses of water and the meaning of life.

And then a friend asked me to join her and another friend for a walk. It was a walk I'd long meant to do, in the hills north of Wellington, but I had never got around to it. I didn't realise at the time it would be the new thing that would be the prequel to so many more unique and novel experiences. I didn't do it because it was new, though. I did it because I needed something to look forward to with people whose company I liked. I did it because it shook me out of a rut.

We all have those long lists of things that we'll do at some indeterminate point in the future. We say we'll do them in 'a couple of months' or 'when the weather gets better'. This then turns into 'after Christmas when everyone gets back from holiday' then 'when things settle down'. And then, just like that, it's winter again, and the thing still hasn't happened. But this time, the walk actually went ahead. The scenery was beautiful and the company excellent. It was enlivening, especially when my bag rolled down a bank and got stuck in a prickly bush. There were also many stairs to climb. So many that, by the end, we had run out of appropriate cuss words to describe them. My poor lazy legs rebelled by acting like slabs of jelly for the last hour of the walk. I also—to this day—have no idea how some of the bag-snatching prickly bush ended up inside my trousers. But it didn't matter. I was happy. It was also extra satisfying to write in my notebook that night that I'd done it. It gave me a small tug of pleasure to mentally cross something off my 'I really must do that one day' list. I felt better that day than I had in a long time.

The literature says that people who spend their money on experiences rather than objects are likely to be happier.[4] The walk had certainly cheered me up more than the foolhardy impulse purchase that was my purple notebook and pen. It makes sense—you look forward to experiences, planning them gives you something to think about beforehand, and you can reminisce about them later. Maybe I needed more experiences to get myself out of my rut? This got me thinking: what else did I want to do that I'd not got around to yet?

The walk had some amazing views. The downside? We were high up. Too high up. I'm a real wuss with heights. In one of his short stories, Edgar Allan Poe wrote about 'The Imp of the Perverse': the urge to do the wrong thing in certain situations. This includes being really high up and, rather than looking away, wondering how it would feel to fall, and secretly wanting to try. Not so for me. My Imp of the Perverse had moved to Timbuktu, leaving the Imp of the Scaredy-cat in its place. When I'm up high, Imp of the Scaredy-cat would much prefer that I lie on the ground in the foetal position and suck my thumb rather than get anywhere close to the edge.

I tried to do a free-fall once. It was 13 metres high, and required falling backward off a narrow plank. Backward! I didn't even want to fall backward into a foam pit at the trampoline park, let alone into what felt like the abyss. The instructors explained that the wedgie-harness I wore would catch me, and then the 'special braking system' would prevent me from going splat. As I waited for my turn, I watched three other people do it. I saw their terrified expressions as they fell, followed by their relief and delight when they realised they would not die. My turn came far too soon. I stood on the thin slab of wood sticking out above the 13-metre drop and closed my eyes, ready to fall at the count of three. But, I didn't. I wouldn't. My body wouldn't let me. Fear flooded my entire being and clouded my brain. I just couldn't do it. The Imp of the Scaredy-cat had surfaced and was here to stay. Instead of falling as I'd paid to do, I scrambled back to the safety of land, took off my wedgie-harness and slunk away.

The walk reminded me of how little I liked heights and how much I wanted to beat the Imp of the Scaredy-cat into submission. One idea I'd had was to go to Adrenalin Forest, a confidence course that weaves through treetops. It sounded like fun, and I'd checked in advance: it took you up high, but there were no free-fall drops. I asked around. Who wants to go to Adrenalin Forest with me? Some said no. Others said it was a great idea, but were busy whenever I suggested it. Three separate people said they would definitely give it a go. But it hadn't happened. The three separate people who would definitely give it a go always had more than three separate reasons not to. It was going to be one of those plans that got talked about for months, but never actually came to pass. At the rate I was going, I wouldn't make it to Adrenalin Forest in the next decade. After a while, I stopped asking. I was embarrassed by how eager I'd been. If someone wanted to go with me, they would have done so by now. It was time to make peace with the fact that, like the 13-metre free-fall, I'd probably never do it.

Speaking of rejections, ever had one of those weeks when you really, *really* want to do something social on a Friday night, but it doesn't go to plan? It doesn't even have to be anything fancy—a made-for-TV movie and a bowl of popcorn will do. Nor does it have to be with anyone particularly special. All you need is a friend: someone you like to talk to, someone who makes you laugh. All you want to do is relax in the company of another human being, rather than be alone. Your resolve not to spend Friday night alone begins to take on a primal life of its own. You can't be alone on Friday, you simply cannot. So you plan a night out dancing, which falls apart, then plan another outing with different people that goes the same way. As a last resort you settle on seeing a movie and ask pretty much every single person you know if they want to join you, and they all say no. Then, on the way home after going to the movie by yourself, you cry, because you counted that you asked 27 people to spend time with you that evening, and not a single person said yes.

Never happened to you? OK, maybe it's just me then. I hope so—I wouldn't wish 27 Rejections of Doom on anyone else.

The week that happened to me, I'd tried so hard to do all of the things you're supposed to do when you're feeling lonely and low. I'd taken all of the advice people give. Put yourself out there! Join a club! Seize the moment! Keep busy! Yet, here I was. Just me, my ice cream and a movie theatre full of couples. Not just any ice cream, either. This was my second. I'd dropped the first one on the floor, fumbling for my phone. Fumbling for my phone and checking for messages that weren't there.

Because this is the story of my year of new things, it's tempting to weave some sort of narrative out of this tale of woe, to recast that lost and lonely evening as the moment everything changed. It wasn't. This was real life, and in real life the realisation that things need to change is usually more of a slow burn than a sudden moment of clarity. If my life were a movie, I would have flicked my hair, made a sassy-yet-charming comment to the person in the ticket booth, and smiled the knowing smile of someone who has just turned their life around. If this were the movies, that night would have been the perfect opening sequence, with music and perfect hair and a certain power in my stride that said, 'I am woman, hear me roar!'

But, alas, life isn't the movies. The 27 Rejections of Doom was a low point, but when you're in the cesspit of despair, you don't have the perspective or ability to think rationally about the situation. You're too busy being sad. There may be a ladder out of the hole you're floundering around in, but who can see it when your eyes are filled with tears? Not to mention the other bits of sticky residue from the cesspit of despair: anger; lethargy; grumpiness; indifference towards things you used to be excited about; an overwhelming desire to eat your body weight in cheese.

I couldn't see the ladder out of the pit. If anything, that evening made me feel worse. My misery and loneliness were overwhelming, and the voice inside my head turned into a heinous bitch-face bully that spewed forth venom: *You are a loser*; *You are shit*; *You have no friends*; *You're ugly*. She's a nasty one, that voice. If it belonged to anyone other than me, I'd go to the police and take out a restraining order.

As I drove home from the movies that night, I thought: *I can't live like this*. But then the heinous bitch-face bully came back, and I wasn't able to think rationally about the situation again for another month. I was too busy doggy-paddling in my cesspit of despair, concentrating with all my might on not going under. I didn't decide to embark on my year of new things for a little while—I couldn't see the ladder up and out of the pit, not yet.

After the 27 Rejections of Doom, to use an overworn cliché, something inside me died. It's impossible to explain your own abject misery to other people. Sadness of that ilk is like breaking a bone or getting your little toe caught in the corner of a door—it hurts like fuck, but you can never quite explain the pain in a way someone else would totally understand. Even if the other person has had similar pain to you, they'll consider the pain to have been worse for them, as they're the one experiencing it. That's why generations of women have turned to their own mothers after giving birth and said, 'You never told me it hurt so much.' Besides, it always sounds so trite to describe that hollow, sad feeling. All of the clichés have already been used: a light going out; a darkness descending; a drowning sorrow. And those words still don't quite capture how lonely and isolating misery can feel, because words are just words, yet the misery is so entrenched in your soul it seems to exist in all four dimensions of time and space. It becomes hard to do the simplest of things, like remembering to buy more milk or take out the recycling on recycling day. My continuous lurking in the cesspit of despair since the night of 27 Rejections of Doom hit me especially hard socially. I was scared to initiate plans to fill the times I didn't have responsibility for the kids, for what if people said no? I didn't need more evidence of my loner loser status, thank you very much. So I didn't reach out to anyone, passively hoping that others would read my mind and invite me places. I'd even throw out meek little hints. Oh, I'd love to see that movie! Oh, I really fancy going for a drink sometime soon! Do you have any plans for the weekend? But no one noticed, or if they did they ignored me. Apart from that walk, no one asked me to do anything with them. They were all too busy living their own lives.

Then—early one week, a friend said she might be keen to go for a walk the following Saturday. Hurrah! A plan! With a friend! The Friday morning before the weekend in question, we'd swapped a few messages online.

'Did you still want to hang out tomorrow?' I said.

Nothing. She was online, but no message came my way. It seemed the conversation was over. *Oh well*, I thought. *She must be busy, or distracted.* There was probably a good explanation. She wouldn't point-blank ignore me. Or would she? No, of course she wouldn't. We wouldn't be friends if she was that sort of person.

Some hours later, a workmate asked me what I was doing that weekend. I looked back at my phone to see whether I had a message. I didn't, although I could see that my friend was online again. A lump formed in my throat. I had no other plans and didn't have the kids, so if the walk didn't happen I'd have nothing else to do. At this late notice, I also had no one else to ask. At that time, my other friends weren't 'let's spontaneously do things tomorrow' friends. They were 'I think I'm free the Wednesday after next but let me check my diary first' friends. They were the sort of friends who needed calendar coordination akin to a military operation before you could see them. Earlier in the week I might have been able to arrange something if I'd managed to muster the confidence, but I hadn't. Now it was too late.

'I don't know what I'm doing yet,' I said to the workmate. 'Probably just having a quiet one.'

'That sounds nice,' my workmate said.

I looked at my feet. My shoes needed a shine. Maybe that's what I'd be doing this weekend instead of going for a walk with a friend. Shining my shoes. Alone.

'Yeah,' I said. 'Nice.'

I messaged the friend again in the early evening when I saw she was online again. I knew I was breaking all etiquette regarding double-messaging and looked desperate. I also knew it was probably a no, but it didn't hurt to check, surely? She might have forgotten. The messages might not have been delivered and there might be some sort of glitch that made messages appear 'seen' when they hadn't been. She might have been hit by a bus and hadn't logged out of Messenger first. Or maybe she'd moved to Mars? Mars with wifi, to explain why she was still online. I had a million and one excuses. Besides, I've never been sure what length of silence is code for 'I'm avoiding actually telling you no, please take the hint'. Is it an hour, half a day, a whole day? I still don't know the answer to that question. I'm an optimist—I'll always think something is a possibility until explicitly told otherwise.

Eventually, a message. 'Sorry. I'll give it a miss.'

So there it was. I looked at my feet again. It's me and you, shoes. This was a moment that would surely make the wrong list when I wrote in my purple notebook that night. I had pinned my Saturday plans on someone who had probably never intended to spend time with me in the first place, and had been non-committal only to be polite. I hadn't heeded the words of Jack Johnson when he sang in 'Flake' that maybe usually means no.

I trudged home in the dark, sad and alone. But as I walked I thought, *This isn't working. This chapter of the script sucks.* Then, an idea: what if I set out to do as many new things as I could, eventually aiming for 52 new things in 52 weeks? Dr Seuss wrote that you can never be bored when you're trying something new. That cold, wintry day, I agreed. I decided I was going to start the very next day by going to Adrenalin Forest. By myself.

Then, things fell into place. I told my sister, and she offered to babysit so Alan could come as well. My sister—in fact my entire family—didn't like the fact that Alan and I had separated. It upset them, because they liked him and didn't understand what the problem was. Not that they would explicitly say so, of course. They didn't want to create problems or dramas. Instead, they did small, subtle things to help get us back on track. Like offering to babysit when I hadn't even asked. I didn't mind. In fact, I was grateful. It was our first adventure together since having children. Maybe there was more to our relationship than bickering about how long the extractor fan ought to run in the bathroom.

As we climbed the trees in dorky-looking harnesses, I pushed myself further out of my comfort zone than I had in years. I hated it. I swore. I screamed. I experienced paralysing fear, and am still counting my lucky stars that I didn't wet myself, high up in those bloody trees. It was that terrifying, and the Imp of the Scaredy-cat was ever present. But afterward I felt proud, happy and strong. I felt like spring was finally coming. My mind whirled with all of the other things I could do. Big, interesting things that would give me something to look forward to. Small things that I could do at home that would give me a feeling of self-satisfaction once they were done.

That night, I stayed up until the wee hours, looking up bucket lists, tourism sites and daily-deal web pages. I asked my friends on Facebook what I should do as part of my new-things challenge and was inundated with ideas, some that never would have occurred to me in a thousand years. Another surprise wasn't the ideas, but the offers: 'I've always wanted to do this, and I'll do it with you. Let's do this together.' I then took it a step further, asking those close to me: 'Is there anything you've always meant to do and not done before? We have a year to do it. I'd love to do a new thing with you.' Also, I made plans with Alan. I owed it to the children to give it another go, to try to rediscover what we'd lost. I needed to remember what made us fall in love in the first place. I'd read about a 1974 psychology study that found that experiencing terror can make other people seem sexier to you.[5] What better excuse to try some downright terrifying things with him?

And the most important things: the things I could do alone. Things that I didn't need anyone else to do with me. I didn't really like the idea of doing things alone, and it was little wonder. I wasn't being terribly kind to myself over that winter; when rattling around in my own mind, I wasn't very good company for myself. But I remembered something I'd forgotten some time ago—that I used to like my own company. I would aim to spend the next year figuring out how to do that again.

I thought that my new things were going to be the magic bullet that would solve all of my problems.

I thought, *I am away.*

# 2

## THE THIRD UGLIEST

✳ **New thing 2:** Having a beauty-counter makeover

✳ **New thing 3:** Having a manicure

✳ **New thing 4:** Getting false eyelashes

✳ **New thing 5:** Having a caricature drawn of myself

✳ **New thing 6:** Wearing bright-red lipstick in public

✳ **New thing 7:** Getting my 'colours' done

✳ **New thing 8:** Going on acne medication

✳ **New thing 9:** Going mountain biking

✳ **New thing 10:** Trying dragon boating

✳ **New thing 11:** Going bouldering

✳ **New thing 12:** Entering a push-up competition

✳ **New thing 13:** Shooting a bow and arrow

**WHEN I WAS FIFTEEN, I WAS** voted the third-ugliest person at school.

Over twenty years have since passed, and rational, adult me knows that I'm not ugly—I have had plenty of men find me attractive, as well as a handful of women. I have aged no better or worse than my peers. My rational, adult self also knows that beauty is both subjective and skin-deep. It's not a mark of character, or of goodness. But being voted third ugliest back at school set me on a painful life course I am only beginning to understand as my thirties draw to a close.

In some ways, the course wasn't so bad.

Feeling ugly made me focus on my mind. I don't want to be pretty anyway, I told myself. I'm smart. I don't want to be like the beautiful bimbos, I said to myself. I'd rather be able to list all of the US states and Wonders of the Ancient World than look good. I also became the 'funny' one, the girl with self-deprecating humour who made people laugh, never mind if it was often at my own expense. I decided that I'd never get a boyfriend anyway, so I might as well just be friends with the boys. I became the girl who was always available to hear about how much they longed for my better-looking friends. I was put in the 'friend zone' years before it became a thing.

These things aren't so bad in retrospect. Deciding to be the 'smart girl' instead of the 'pretty girl' has meant that I am ageing much more comfortably than women I know whose looks defined them when we were younger. I still value laughing—it's one of my favourite pastimes, and makes situations easier to bear. Not being image-conscious is often more fun, as there is a certain freedom in not caring about looking like a dork. I've never minded doing things like my **new thing 51**, spontaneously entering a public dance competition, even though I didn't know any of the moves so danced like I was alone in my living room instead of on a stage in Federation Square. Being in the 'friend zone' before it even had a name doesn't just make me a trend-setter who was cool well before my time. It also means I can develop satisfying platonic friendships with men without getting daft about it. My two closest confidants are men. Besides, working from the assumption that someone doesn't see you as 'more than a friend' unless they explicitly tell you otherwise frees up headspace for more important matters. Such as: what came first, the chicken or the egg? Did Steven Avery do it? And which is more delicious, pink or white marshmallows?

And yet . . . Sticks and stones may break your bones but words echo around your soul forever.

I know I'm not alone. We women often worry about how we look and what we weigh. Body insecurity is a legacy that can get passed down through the generations, especially from mother to daughter. Men are often insecure about their bodies, too. In *Adulthood for Beginners*, Andy Boyle talks openly about his own battle with his self-image, and finding that losing weight wasn't the self-esteem fix he thought it would be. He concludes: 'you'll always think something is a little wrong with it [your body]. That's just how we're wired.'[1] Analysis of Google Ads shows that 42 per cent of clicks on ads relating to fitness and beauty are carried out by men, as well as 39 per cent of clicks related to cosmetic surgery.[2]

I know men who hate how they look, and the only person I know who has body dysmorphia is a man. I think it's worse for women, though. When I was voted the third ugliest at school, numbers one through five were all girls. It wasn't that the boys at school were made in the image of Adonis—they were normal gangly, spotty, smelly teenage boys. Yet it was only the girls who came under the microscope.

This heightened focus on girls' appearances is common. While 28 per cent of girls are classified as overweight, 35 per cent of boys are—yet parents are twice as likely to ask Google how to help their daughters to lose weight than ask a similar question about their sons.[3] My girlfriends often talk about what is wrong with their bodies and faces, using words to describe themselves that would be classed as verbal abuse if they came from anyone else. It's as if we've collectively shrugged our shoulders and accepted that self-loathing is part and parcel of being a woman. Blaming the media or men or cosmetics companies doesn't help the insecure fifteen-year-old girl when she looks in the mirror and hates what she sees. Knowing that other people felt bad about how they looked didn't make me feel any better about myself, and the implications of that vote haunted me for years.

For a long time, I dressed conservatively, lest I be noticed. I hid behind glasses. I didn't like wearing anything bright, floral or a bit different. When someone complimented how I looked, I wondered if they were making fun of me. I wore minimal make-up—not because I wanted to, but because I didn't want to make an effort. I was self-sabotaging. I didn't want to try in case I got it wrong and ended up looking like a kid who had snuck into her mother's bedroom, had a play with her lippy and emerged looking like a clown.

When I was a teenager I told a close friend I had feelings for him. He was one of my best friends—we talked and laughed together and enjoyed each other's company. But he wasn't interested; he was in the process of falling for someone else. He didn't see me 'like that'. I asked him what she was like, this other girl. 'I am so attracted to her,' he replied. Those words reminded me of who I was. I was the girl you laugh with, talk with and enjoy the company of, but I was still the third ugliest.

I knew I needed to break out of the 'one of the lads' dynamic with some of the men in my life, but it went against the habit of two decades. Several years ago, at my gym, I was spending a lot of time with a group of men who didn't think anything of talking about women they found attractive in front of me. I was party to conversations about blondes versus brunettes and which ethnic groups are hottest. I didn't want these men to fancy me, but I still felt bad about myself when they talked about how attractive they found other women. I never once told them how uncomfortable and downright hideous the whole topic made me feel. It didn't occur to me. All I heard was a constant reminder that I was not in the camp of women they were talking about. I was reminded of being fifteen, and the boy I liked telling me how much he liked someone else because she was so pretty.

In spite of having near-perfect skin since my teens, I'd recently developed the horrendous condition that is adult acne. Acne is horrible. It may affect 20–54 per cent of the population,[4] but knowing that doesn't make it any easier when you've got a particularly bad case and have no idea why your near-perfect skin has suddenly turned into a homage to Mount Vesuvius. No amount of expensive face wash or not eating chocolate or face masks or the milk of Himalayan mountain goats as fetched by virginal yaks cleared it up.

The difference between pimples and acne is like the difference between a common cold and the flu: some people conflate the two, but they are not the same at all. One is painful but bearable, but the other knocks the wind out of your sails more than you can possibly imagine unless you've experienced it yourself. I wasn't surprised to read that, according to studies, the impacts of acne can include feelings of shame, anger, lack of pride and impaired self-image.[5] When you have acne, you feel like your body hates you. Waking up some mornings is like a game of Russian roulette—where will I have a big ugly spot today? I don't know how other adult-acne sufferers feel, but it left me feeling deeply ashamed.

Even now, writing about acne is *much* harder than writing about having been overweight. Talking about it makes me feel vulnerable, even with the benefit of hindsight and clearer skin. The sense of shame still lingers. It ate me up. How can you hold your head high and walk into a room full of people when you know that head is covered in ugly red spots? My shame was so deep I barely spoke to anyone else about it, including other people who had problem skin. Dieting and body image are discussed often; people swap theories, talk about their goals and provide communal support. I can natter about diets all day and not feel bad about myself, but skin is different. You feel dirty. You feel disgusting. You feel frustrated and angry that you've tried everything you can think of, but nothing works. When you have acne, you notice people trying not to look at your spots. Even if they're not looking, you think that they are: you feel that every spot is accompanied by a giant sparkly arrow pointing right at the head of the beast. My rational self understands that this is what Thomas Gilovich dubbed 'the spotlight effect'—the misconception that other people notice everything about you when they are most likely thinking about other things.[6] Like themselves. I wanted it to be true that it was all in my head, but I still felt like the spotlight was pointed right at me. I felt looked at and judged. While you may know that acne is hormonal and can't be helped, you still assume that people think you never wash your face and that you need to drink more water. It's embarrassing and, because it's your face, it can't be hidden, unless by a balaclava. I stopped wearing glasses when my skin got worse, as being the bespectacled spotty girl felt too close to my fifteen-year-old third-ugliest self. The comments people made when I stopped wearing glasses made things worse. Constant comments, from what felt like everyone I saw on a day-to-day basis. I didn't like it. I preferred to pretend that people didn't notice me at all. *If they notice my glasses, of course they notice my spots*, I thought. I felt deeply betrayed by the looks gods. You're not supposed to have acne, wrinkles and grey hair all at once. I wanted to throw my toys and cry like a toddler: it's not FAIR!

During my year of new things, I decided to make more of an effort. I hate the phrase 'let yourself go', especially when it's applied to women who have had children. But I had. It was true. At first it made sense to let myself go. I was tired. Activewear was so comfortable. And what was the point of wearing nice things, only to have them covered in the bodily fluids of a small child? It felt ridiculously decadent to spend money on myself, especially on beauty treatments and clothes I didn't need. But the baby years were behind me, and shuffling around in unflattering clothes wasn't doing my self-esteem any favours. It was time to change—to restore my pre-child self, and to confront my third-ugliest demons.

I started dressing more bravely, but still felt shy. In my mind I was an imposter, a little kid who was playing grown-up. Even when I was looking my best, sometimes, when looking in the mirror, I still saw my fifteen-year-old self looking back. Being noticed—my hair, my clothes, my face—mortified me, as it reminded me that people observe these things. Whenever anyone said I was looking trimmer or my hair was shinier, I wondered, *Did they think I looked fat and dowdy before?* I would have happily lived my life with a paper bag over my head with holes cut out for eyes, but people would have noticed that too, so it would have defeated the purpose.

Early in my year of new things, I read Roxane Gay's 'memoir' of her body, *Hunger*. She wrote: 'I don't want to change who I am. I want to change how I look. On my better days, when I feel up to the fight, I want to change how this world responds to how I look because intellectually I know my body is not the real problem. On bad days, though, I forget how to separate my personality, the heart of who I am, from my body.'[7] This resonated with me; I too had forgotten how to separate my personality from my body.

I remained on the search for the one potion that would repair my self-esteem. While hunting for these products, the very act of going into department stores to buy make-up preyed on my deepest insecurities. The bright lights and mirrors conspired to make me painfully aware of every blemish on my face, something I was particularly self-conscious about. Mirror, mirror on the wall, who's the third-ugliest of them all? As if the bright lights and mirrors weren't enough, I was confronted with 6235 different types of concealer to cover my pimples, all in different types of packaging with different textures. God only knew what was supposed to work. It was like being a person at their first banquet, looking down at the half-dozen knives and forks in front of them, not knowing where to start—but even worse, because there was no simple rule to adhere to like 'start at the outside and work your way in'. Instead there were confusing words like 'contouring' and 'highlights' and 'primer'. That was just for the skin, not to mention the eyes, with all the eyeshadows, dozens of colours of liner, and the stuff that is supposed to make you look less tired by applying it under your eyes.

And the biggest change since I was a teenager: the eyebrows. Turns out they are now bigger than *Ben-Hur*. What used to be a case of simple plucking is now an ideological divide: the pencil or the powder? I asked a shop assistant if I could see some eyeliner. Which sort? she asked. Black, I said. No, she said, which sort? She then motioned towards a dozen black eyeliners that were apparently quite different in spite of looking exactly the same. I did what I often do in such situations: looked at my watch and muttered something about a meeting before scuttling away. *I don't belong in such places*, I thought. *They aren't for people like me.* They were only for the sort of women that my male friends would ogle when we were out at bars.

But this was my year of new things. I wanted to try new things to become a new me, and I wanted that new version of myself to look better. I wanted to learn how not to be the third-ugliest girl anymore. So, I did something that terrified me: for **new thing 2**, I braved a beauty-counter makeover.

It took a number of visits to the department store to summon the courage. I'd slink in, casually browse, then scuttle away when a sales assistant asked if they could help. Then one day, I finally bit the bullet and booked a session. As soon as the words were out of my mouth I wanted to run and hide somewhere far from all of the face potions, but I gave myself a stern talking to. I was going to do it. It terrified me, but how else would I feel better about myself?

As I mounted the stool, the voice in my head said, *You don't belong there. Nothing can fix you. You're making a fool of yourself.* The voice recited the greatest hits of the other excuses I'd used over the years to not learn how to apply make-up properly: *You're being a bad feminist; there is no point in wearing make-up; this is a waste of money; you're vain and no one likes a vain person.* Then the voice in my head got warmed up and went in for the kill. It said, *The lady doing your make-up knows you're a lost cause.* I wasn't having any of that inner voice that day, though. I'd committed to do my new things, and this was to be one of them. If my new things were easy they wouldn't teach me anything. I told my inner voice to bugger off and pretended to look comfortable while the lovely woman with the brushes weaved her magic.

'It's art,' she said as she applied goop to my face. 'I used to want to be a conventional artist, but I like doing this more.'

'Why?'

'Because it makes more people happy.'

Art. Huh. I'd never thought of it like that before. And the result was impressive, for the colours were just right. I got the woman to talk me through what she was doing, and returned the next day for further instructions. I learned tips and tricks that I could do at home.

Initially, it did wonders for my confidence. The more I hung out at beauty counters after my makeover, the less I felt like an imposter. I talked to friends who loved make-up and surprised myself by how much I enjoyed the art of make-up application: the difference in effect between a roll-on eye shadow and a powder, the subtle difference in the way the various eyeliners looked, and the ease of application. Maybe this wasn't so scary after all.

After the makeover, I was full of ideas about the other new things I could do to make myself feel better. Many of these were things that other women do often and don't think anything of. For me, though, they were all things I hadn't tried because doing them didn't conform to the sort of woman I thought I was. For **new thing 3** I had my first manicure, shyly choosing coral colours that barely looked any different from my natural nails. I'd never really painted my nails—I thought that manicures weren't for women like me, and whenever I'd tried to do it myself it looked like I'd stirred a tin of Dulux paint with my fingers. I loved the manicure, though, and booked another one right away. By the end of the year I was wearing brighter colours. One week I was grumpy and sad, so had my nails painted electric blue. It cheered me up more than I'd ever thought possible, a little pick-me-up gift that kept on giving every time I looked at my hands. It wasn't for anyone else; it was for me. I'd had no idea how much better it would make me feel; if I'd known, I would have had a manicure years ago.

I had false eyelashes professionally applied for **new thing 4**. For all my insecurity about beauty counters, mascara was the one product I'd worn since the age of fourteen, when I realised it stopped my eyes looking like they were being eaten by my face. After over twenty years of mascara application and the ever-present risk of panda eyes, it seemed like a logical new thing to try.

I was nervous. False eyelashes don't conjure up images of subtle beauty. When I thought 'false eyelashes', I thought of women with what looked like spiders glued to their eyelids. I didn't want spider eyes, so begged the woman doing the application for 'the natural look', hoping that she didn't think 'natural' meant 'an arachnid in its natural habitat'. It wasn't a terribly comfortable procedure, getting the eyelashes glued on. It took the lady three goes to attach my lower lashes to my cheeks with what felt like sellotape. Then, this instruction:

'Whatever you do, do not open your eyes!' You'd think I would welcome lying on a bed for 90 minutes with my eyes closed. But no. Being told you simply cannot do a thing just makes you want to do it. Lying with my eyes closed was surprisingly difficult, especially while someone hovered above me touching my eyelids. It would have been easier if the woman had said, 'Whatever you do, don't go to sleep!'

When the woman finished and handed me the mirror, I was overcome with fear. Would I have to find a paper bag with slits for eyes to cover my shame? Had I made a terrible mistake? But I hadn't. I loved the effect. There wasn't a spider to be seen, and my lashes looked fabulous. Best of all, it was super convenient. No more eye make-up! No more black streaks on my cheeks if I had a coughing fit or was caught in the rain! In the weeks after my false lashes were put on, I could sleep for a precious extra five minutes in the morning. Ridiculous vanity and year of new things for the win! I'd tried something new, and didn't see any downside whatsoever. There were downsides, though. I just hadn't realised it yet. More on that later.

Pushing myself even further out of my comfort zone about my looks, for **new thing 5** I had a caricature drawn. It's deeply uncomfortable to sit still while someone studies your face through narrowed eyes. In many ways, it wasn't so different from the beauty-counter makeover, although instead of looking for ways to minimise my flaws, the person doing the studying was thinking about how to emphasise them for comic effect. As the man drew, my dastardly inner voice came back, that bastard that gave me a hard time during my beauty-counter makeover.

It was more pitiful this time, silently begging the artist to be kind. *Please don't draw my acne*, it said. *Please don't make me look fat. Oh my God, this was a mistake, what am I doing, I hate this, I want to go home and watch Netflix, this sucks!* Every time a passerby stopped to watch, I regretted that I was paying $20 for something so stupid. I should have bought some ice cream instead. This was the dumbest idea I'd had since the time I got a jumping photo taken while wearing a handbag that flew up and hit me in the face mid-jump. When I'm scared, I often become a rage-beast about totally unrelated things. Random things, as those are easier to focus on than the thing actually scaring the bejeezus out of me. During my failed 13-metre free-fall, I rage-beasted in my mind about someone chewing gum loudly. While up high for **new thing 1**, doing a confidence course through the treetops at Adrenalin Forest, my rage-beastliness was so intense I used swears I didn't know formed part of my vocabulary. As I got my caricature drawn for **new thing 5**, it was some nearby music that made the rage-beast red haze descend.

The artist handed me the giant laminated picture, and all of a sudden the nearby music didn't bother me anymore. He hadn't drawn my acne, and had given me great eyelashes. Thanks, **new thing 4**, the eyelash extensions!

When I got home, I showed the caricature to my kids. Six-year-old Jack got upset.

'That's not you!' he said. 'Put it away. I never want to see that again.'

I was pleased. For all of my bravado, if my son had said, 'Wow, it looks just like you,' I probably would have cried.

46

The year of new things moved forward. For **new thing 6**, I wore bright red lipstick in public. Bright red lips—'party lips'—are an inconsequential thing for so many women. They wear them all of the time, without a second thought. I had spent years envying these confident beings. For the girl previously voted the third-ugliest at school, to draw such attention to myself was the stuff of nightmares. Ever heard the phrase 'lipstick on a pig'? That's what I was scared of—that I was the pig. I thought I would look silly at best and comical at worst. My friend was aghast when I told her I'd never worn bright red lippy.

'You have to!' she said. 'You can't party without party lips!'

In the spirit of the year of new things, I agreed. It took me three visits to two stores to decide what shade of red to buy, as if any variation of bright red was any less obvious, and I obsessed over which lip-liner to get. When I finally settled on a colour, I took the lipstick home and tried it on three more times before I got the nerve to wear it out. Two of my friends, those confident beings who wore bright red lipstick as a matter of course, joined me.

I felt great. Not because it looked particularly good (I still don't think it suits me), but because wearing bright red lipstick—wearing something so *obvious*—proved that I didn't need to be afraid. No one laughed at me, or even looked twice. Not a single person gave a single fuck. I'd been so insecure for so long, I'd turned something really simple—wearing red lipstick—into this massive psychological barrier that was disproportionate to the actual facts of the matter. It was like the spotlight effect on speed. I felt a little silly for having cared so much.

**New thing 7** was getting my colours done. It felt so ridiculous and so 1980—something for the likes of Bridget Jones's mother, not me. I got the idea from a friend who'd had it done herself and now wears bright yellow to work. Yellow to work! In my world of black-clad bureaucrats, wearing yellow into the office was like wearing faux reindeer antlers on Christmas Eve— everyone likes the idea in theory, but no one actually does it. Maybe I'd be brave enough to wear yellow, too? No, that was too ambitious. I'd settle with being brave enough to stray from black and brown and grey and navy blue. The brochure for the colour consultation claimed I would 'rediscover myself'. *Good luck*, I thought. Rediscover what?

A woman draped in scarves arrived at my house in a cloud of perfume. She sat me down for 'the draping'. This sounded ominous, like some sort of ancient ritual required to enter a secret club. 'The draping' involved sitting in front of a mirror without make-up on, watching as she held a variety of coloured fabrics up to my face and studied the effect they had. Silver or gold? Cream or white? This purple or the other purple, even though they looked pretty much the same to me and—as I said at the beginning of this book—I have an irrational hatred of purple. It was mortifying and fascinating all at once. Mortifying because it's weird sitting and looking at yourself in the mirror for an hour while a stranger fusses around you, yet fascinating because the colours really did make a difference. So many times over the years I've seen a photo of myself in something I thought looked nice, but I actually looked washed-out and tired. There were also the times I'd bought a new article of clothing, but never really felt that new-clothes buzz when I wore it. Whenever that happened I'd felt bad, but wasn't surprised. *Of course I don't look that good in the photo*, I would think. *Of course the beautiful tan silk shirt doesn't look good on me.* What else could I expect? I was the third-ugliest girl, and she's not the sort of woman who can wear those sorts of clothes. Whenever something new didn't quite work for me, I thought it was because you couldn't put lipstick on a pig.

Well, that was a filthy self-defeating lie of epic proportions. There was a common denominator whenever that happened, and it wasn't my face. It was the colours I was wearing. When the colours lady rummaged through my wardrobe, the beautiful tan silk shirt was the first thing she put in the 'do not wear' pile. She divided the colour groups into three: the colours I look best in, colours I can wear but don't give me a 'lift', and colours I shouldn't wear at all. The colours she recommended I wear were my favourite colours in the world: bright blue, hot pink, apple green, natural red. But I'd never worn them before; they were too bright for me. It was the lipstick-on-a-pig complex again.

Getting my colours done gave me the confidence I'd always lacked. I overhauled my wardrobe as much as my budget would allow, researching colour and fabric and cuts that suited me, and buying more dresses than one woman ought to own. This included dresses in bright colours that I would never have touched with a barge pole a year earlier. After a little while I didn't even care that they were 'my' colours. All that mattered was that it made me happy to wear them, in a way hiding in conservative black shirts and shapeless skirts had never done in the past.

When the next winter came and it was cold and wet, wearing bright colours made me feel much better than darker tones ever had. An unexpected consequence: Dahla, who was four at the time, was delighted. I'd started wearing the same colours as her. Like all small children, she hadn't yet developed the hang-ups that make most grown-ups eschew bright colours. When we both wore our hot pink sweaters, we were 'twins'. Jack didn't want to be left out, either. He was pleased when I bought a burgundy coat the same colour as his favourite tracksuit bottoms. We were 'twins' as well. For the first time in my life, clothes became fun.

Lastly, for **new thing 8**, I went to the doctor about my skin. Nothing else was working: giving up sugar, cutting back dairy, toners and scrubs and masks and exfoliations. Drinking more water just meant needing to pee all the time, then looking at my spots again in the giant mirror while I washed my hands. The new make-up helped with coverage, but there is only so much you can do to disguise a mountainous terrain.

The doctor took one look at me and prescribed medication that worked, slowly and surely. I had to be patient, but over the year, my skin did improve. Halfway through the year, I realised I hadn't had a terrible spot for a little while. And I realised I wasn't self-conscious about my skin anymore. In fact, I was not self-conscious at all. I felt better about my appearance than I had in my entire life. And not only did I feel better, but I felt a subtle shift in how people treated me. I got little compliments from people I hadn't seen for a while.

'Wow, look at you,' said a former colleague I hadn't seen in years.

'You've transformed,' someone else said.

Another time, a man I vaguely knew turned to another man beside him. 'You wouldn't have recognised Lauren a few years ago,' he said. 'She had glasses and didn't wear dresses and her hair was always tied back.' The second man gave me a look that made me uncomfortable. I wasn't sure if it was a compliment or not.

'You look great,' someone else said. 'Not that you looked bad before. You just looked like you didn't care.'

*Like I didn't care.* I wanted to tell them that I had always cared. Of course I had. It was more complicated than that. I didn't know where to start, though. I didn't know how to explain how deep my third-ugliest demons dwelled. I felt protective of me-of-before, who had only wanted to be invisible, not to give the impression that she didn't care.

'Thanks,' I said instead.

The most obvious difference was shop assistants—they'd linger around me for longer, and take more of an interest in what I was looking at. I'd be trying on clothes and feel like I was in a different club. For the first time in my life, I would go back to a store a week after being there initially, and the shop assistant would remember me. I got more attention from men, and women I barely knew would compliment me on my clothes. On the odd occasion, a complete stranger would say something as well.

'I love that dress!' a woman said once on the street. I glowed for the rest of the day.

Was it because I walked taller, or because I actually looked better? Were the shop assistants just being nicer because I looked like more of a sucker who would spend lots of money? I don't know. It's one of those things that's impossible to unpick—when you're confident, you present a different self to the world, so the world treats you differently. It's impossible to know what came first. It didn't worry me initially. I felt like I occupied a different corner of the world than I had before; a place where you are more likely to command a different type of attention. And for the first little while, I loved it.

But then I realised that I hadn't addressed my issues. Under the bright red lipstick and colours that made me 'pop', I didn't really feel better at all.

The beauty industry is a double-edged sword.

While I felt better than before and had more confidence, I was spending far too much money on products and clothes I didn't need. For a few months, when it was all new and exciting, I became obsessed, constantly trying new items and letting myself be sold potions and lotions that were never going to address the root cause of my insecurities. I may have developed enough confidence to have views on the eyebrow pencil versus powder ideological divide (powder!), but I didn't find that magic product to fix my self-esteem. Over the course of a few months, the needle swung from insecurity to a version of vanity that I hardly recognised in myself. I had hated how

I had looked before, but had held a deep-seated belief that, apart from my weight, I could not change. Alongside my self-loathing about my appearance had sat a version of helplessness that meant I'd trained myself to not even think about how I looked unless it was strictly necessary.

But I was no longer helpless. I now knew that I could change and improve my appearance. The woman who had done my manicure had said: 'There are no ugly women, just lazy women.' I thought this was a bit harsh as I knew first-hand it was far more complicated than simply being 'lazy', but at that time I saw where she was coming from, for I was much more aware of the little tweaks I could make to improve myself. I now knew what a difference basic education about products and their application could make. I spent too much time looking up ideas for what else I could do, for there was always something. And once you start trying to alter your face, where do you stop? I didn't want my interest in make-up to lead to some sort of procedure that would make me look embalmed.

There were also many downsides to some of my vain new ideas. The cost, for one. Make-up isn't cheap. Especially when I was buying bright red lipstick and lip-liner that I only wore twice—once for my party lips in public, and the second time dotted all over my face for a fancy-dress party dressed as someone with the pox. There were other downsides as well. Take the false eyelashes. I loved the effect as well as the extra snooze time, and after changing to a more experienced lash-lady I looked forward to my sessions; I enjoyed the chance to lie on my back, close my eyes and have a gossip with the woman applying them. But they caused all my natural lashes to fall out. I spent a fortnight with one eye that looked glam, and the other looking like a spider with most of its legs pulled out. Because of this—and the fact I have tiny eyes—I felt the need to keep going back as I couldn't stand the bald-lashes look. This was expensive and annoying and time-consuming and not what I'd signed up for. Every few weeks I'd resolve to never get them again because I am a strong, independent woman who should not be addicted to the beauty industry, but after a few days with an eye as bald as Dr Evil's cat, I'd slink back to the salon. Now, whenever friends ask if they should try falsies, I tell them to think *very* carefully about it. I've since been told it can take up to nine months for your lashes to go back to normal. Nine months! I can grow a person in that time. That's just ridiculous. It wasn't that bad for me due to the miracle invention that is eyelash serum, but I did spend at least a month looking like my face was eating my eyes. I've never regretted stopping. I feel free—free of a heavy, fluttery shackle that hadn't even existed a year prior.

Getting my colours done also had a flipside. I loved the confidence it gave me; I wore more colour than ever before, which consistently lifted my mood and made me feel fabulous. But as part of getting my colours done, I was also told what didn't suit me. Not very subtly, either. The stylish lady draped in scarves rummaged through my wardrobe, threw a pile of clothes on the bed and decreed: thou must not wear these things. Her tone implied that, if I did, the fashion gods would cause me to spontaneously combust. As a rule, the clothes I owned in the now-forbidden colours were ones that never made me feel my best anyway—I'd just never realised the colour was the reason why. I'd been too busy hating myself to pay attention to what colours worked or didn't work. Case in point: the tan silk shirt. But the pile of doom included my favourite scarf. I loved that scarf. I had bought it on a shopping trip with Mum, right before I went back to work after maternity leave. It is tan and cream and covered in sunflowers, my favourite flower. When I wore it, it made me think of the lovely time I'd had with my mum that day, the cake we had eaten, the nervous feeling of going back to work after some time off, and the delight in having something lovely to wear. The scarf used to make me happy, but didn't anymore. Whenever I wore it, I felt a bit naughty, like I was doing something wrong. It didn't bring me joy like it used to, which I knew to be ridiculous, but I couldn't help it. I had to consciously remind myself that you don't have to look your best all of the time. Sometimes it's nice to wear something because it has nice memories attached or you like the pattern, not because it matches your skin tone.

I started to feel bad about things that had never worried me before. My handbag became so heavy with my emergency cosmetic supplies I'm lucky I didn't hurt my arm lugging it all around. When I didn't care about what I wore each day, dressing was easy. Now I had so many options, I spent more time trying to decide what to wear, especially if I had something on that day that made me nervous. I worried about the lesson I was teaching Dahla as I came home with a new pair of shoes, a new dress or a new shade of lipstick. I realised I was modelling a side of stereotypical womanhood I didn't necessarily want her to emulate.

I wanted things I could not afford, procedures that went beyond simple make-up application. There was so much more that I could do to improve myself, things that involved needles and surgery and UV lights and all manner of other expensive things. A beauty-counter makeover, a manicure, fake lashes and wearing party lips in public were only the tip of the iceberg. I felt better about my appearance, but I wasn't completely comfortable with the vainer version of myself that I had become. I loved the extra attention, but missed the version of myself that didn't waste so much money. Sometimes I missed the version of myself that thought that your looks couldn't change so there was no point in trying. It was hard to consciously draw a line under my quest for self-improvement and say: I'm done now. I have to stop. This is enough.

One Friday, I went out with a group of friends. It was supposed to have been a drink after work but somehow turned into the wrong side of midnight, dancing to 1980s pop music in an underground club. I was having a fabulous time dancing, chatting and laughing. I felt my best that night. I was wearing my favourite dress, and my make-up was expertly applied thanks to the tips I'd learned during my makeover. The medication for my skin had begun to take effect. Maybe, just maybe, I wasn't the third-ugliest girl anymore.

I bumped into an old uni friend of mine, who on this particular evening was suffering from that toxic combination of having had too much to drink and a broken heart—his on/ off relationship with the girl he'd described as 'really hot and the whole package' had recently been turned off. He was drunk and distracted, and kept looking around at other women. I had lost my other friends and didn't want to be left alone. An aggressive-looking drunk man was circling me, and I knew he'd leave me alone only as long as my friend was there.

'Can you stay here with me?' I asked.

His eyes followed a blonde girl around the room.

'It's fine as long as there aren't any hot girls around,' he said. He looked at the blonde girl again. 'Actually, I'm going to go and talk to her.'

I closed my eyes. A wave of nausea hit me. 'Maybe I should go home.'

'Don't be silly,' he said. 'But don't play yourself off against the hot girls.'

It was one of those moments when, for want of a less cheesy line, time stood still. For some reason, my first thought was of the hair lotion my hairdresser had convinced me to buy last week, which I'd used for the first time the previous evening. It was such a waste of money. Hurt and self-loathing surged through my veins. Girls like me needed more than hair lotion to run through their locks. I remembered something a younger relative had once said when I was a teenager: you fell down the ugly tree and your face hit every branch. I didn't care about my friend. I just cared that, once again, I was put in the wrong category of woman. I was the friend who was only good for passing time with until a hot girl came along. I had been trying to be different, but I wasn't. It was like lipstick on a pig.

I left for home right away, devastated. My dress felt drab, my efforts farcical. I thought about all of my spots and wrinkles and blemishes with hatred, and cried in the taxi on the way home. As it happened, the taxi passed the big, shiny make-up shop where I had bought my bright-red lipstick. Sitting in the back of that taxi, the sight of the place made me cry even harder. *I tried so hard and spent so much money and I was still not one of the hot girls*, I thought. I was still the girl who fills a gap when the pretty girls aren't around. I hadn't changed at all. My life wasn't like a Hollywood movie where the awkward nerdy girl takes off her glasses and flicks her hair and suddenly looks hot. I was the awkward nerdy girl who took off her glasses and flicked her hair but was still the awkward nerdy girl, just without glasses. That night, I couldn't think of a single thing that could have hurt me more.

I was also angry at the people who had called me ugly in the first place, at society for placing such a premium on beauty, and at the department stores for having such bright lights and ridiculously large mirrors everywhere. I was angry that I now owned four types of black eye-liner when none of them suited me anyway. But, most importantly, I was angry at myself for letting such a stupid thing affect me as much as it had. I had done my new things. I'd had my beauty-counter makeover, got my false lashes, worn my bright-red lipstick and let a caricature artist study my face. These things all pushed me out of my comfort zone and I do not regret a single one, but they weren't enough. I was never going to find that magic potion to repair my self-esteem. I was never going to find it unless I changed direction.

Over the following weeks, I decided what to do.

First, I would stop putting myself in situations that were bad for my sense of self-worth. I was not going to be the 'cool girl' who smiles and nods when men objectified women in front of me any longer. Such behaviour is abhorrent and gross, and I had failed the sisterhood by not calling it out. Besides, it was terrible for my own happiness. I didn't need to be told that I shouldn't play myself off against the hot girls in the room. No single product was going to fix my self-esteem if I continued to put myself in situations where I let people say such things to me. And this wasn't just true for men—there were plenty of examples when women had been just as brutal, albeit in a subtler way. The 'friend' who said she always admired how I was 'comfortable' in my body, the person who called my initial attempts to do make-up 'cute'. The workmate who commented on every single tweak I made to my appearance: 'Where are your glasses? You look so different!'; 'You're wearing high heels? You never wear high heels!' and so on and so forth. These people weren't worth my time. Life is too short to spend time with people who make you feel bad about yourself. My own inner voice of self-doubt gives me enough of a hard time. I don't need external people to give it any ammunition.

Second, I would be a better role model for Dahla. She had recently turned four, but was already far more aware of her appearance than I was comfortable with. Like most mothers, I had tried my very hardest to shield her from my own neuroses, but influences were already seeping in—from society, from the media and from me. She had once cried because she didn't have 'beautiful' white hair like Elsa in *Frozen*, and asked why the girls with long hair at day care didn't like her and was it because her hair was short? When she had chickenpox, I found her standing in front of the mirror, examining her spots.

'What's wrong, darling?' I said, trying to give her a cuddle. She pulled away.

'I'm not beautiful,' she said. 'I'm ugly.'

'You're not ugly.'

'Yes, I am,' she said sadly. 'Look at my spots.'

'But spots aren't ugly. You're still beautiful.'

She narrowed her eyes. 'You're lying. You think spots are ugly.'

I hung my head. The blame was mine. Of course she thought being spotty equated to being ugly—she'd heard me complaining to Alan about my acne. I needed to develop a better relationship with my own looks for her sake. Feeling like the third-ugliest girl could not be a mantle that got passed down the generations. I needed my legacy to my daughter to be one of body confidence.

Lastly, I needed to care less about my outward appearance, and focus on what my body could do, rather than how it looked. I'd known this all along, deep down. Don't we all? But it was time to try to put it into practice. In the film *Within the Whirlwind* (2009), the character Evgenia Ginzburg loosely quotes Russian poet Osip Mandelstam, when she says: 'Somebody gave me this body; what do I do with it now? It's a very remarkable body, and nobody's body but mine. I'm alive and I breathe, I'm strong and tall. Won't somebody tell me who to thank for it all?'[8] Mandelstam was right. My body is nobody's but mine, and it's remarkable. I'm alive and I breathe, and, all going to plan, I intend to continue doing so for some time to come. I'm lucky. Mandelstam wasn't so lucky; he died in a gulag in Russia's Far East in 1938, which certainly puts my complaints into perspective. It was time for me to be less vain. I'm able-bodied, have functional limbs and no serious health concerns. My new things needed to reflect that.

I've never been particularly athletic. I'm not built for exercise—I am too wobbly in all of the wrong places and not blessed in the coordination department. I played hockey when I was eleven. Mum said she'd pay me 10 cents whenever I hit the ball. I didn't make more than 50 cents the entire season, and that was pity money. Having hyper-mobile joints doesn't help my physical endeavours, either. My joints have a larger range of motion than they are supposed to, and because of this I—literally—cannot walk in a straight line. I walk in little zigzags instead. I trained for and ran a half-marathon when I was in my late twenties, but, because of my joints, I injured my feet so badly I couldn't walk without pain for months. It took years to come right, and I've not had the confidence in my body to try something that pushes me that hard since.

At the beginning of the year of new things, my lack of fitness was shocking. My only exercise over the winter was running for the bus. You can remind yourself a hundred million times that fresh air and exercise are good for mental health, but when times are bad it's almost impossible to get the motivation to do it. In hard times, you're too busy surviving to go for a run or swim or bike or water polo or whatever else tickles your fancy. It's what I think of as the Downward Spiral of Suck— that when you're unhappy, the things that make you feel better are the hardest things to do. And the things that can ultimately make you feel worse—like eating an entire packet of biscuits in one sitting or spending a sunny Saturday with a raging hangover instead of getting outside—are easier to do. Why the Downward Spiral of Suck? Because it sucks.[9]

Indeed, I was terribly unfit. But the path to body confidence is paved with feeling strong, not feeling pretty. It was time to start doing things that pushed me physically.

**New thing 9** was going mountain biking. I live at the base of a mountain-bike park, so my suburb is overrun by that mysterious tribe of people who ride around covered in mud and drop terms like 'shock absorbers' and 'grade-A track' into conversations. It was a beautiful day, so off I went to hire a bike.

I loved it. On the way up, I biked under the trees, listened to the birdsong from the native birds, and felt an inner peace of the sort one cannot write about without sounding cheesier than cheese sauce. On the way down I felt like a speed demon, although was actually so slow I held up a couple of other people on the track. Turns out my sense of being a speed demon is someone else's Old Lady on a Sunday Drive in a Lada. Never mind. My body is no one's but mine, and it's a body that can mountain bike. I liked it so much, it became a hobby. I've since bought my own mountain bike. I'm still no speed demon, but I don't cause traffic jams on the track anymore either.

For **new thing 10**, I tried dragon boating. It was hard and wet and exhilarating. As I paddled in unison with a boat of strangers, the burning in my arms was akin to being prodded with white-hot pokers. I couldn't stop, though, because I didn't want to be the fool who accidentally makes the boat go in circles. The guy sitting beside me said he trained by lifting jugs of beer to his mouth. Maybe that would have helped. Afterward, when I lifted a can of Coke Zero to take a sip, my biceps wobbled so much I missed my mouth. Maybe I did need to train by lifting heavier drinks—then maybe I wouldn't have got Coke Zero down the front of my T-shirt. Not that it mattered. I was sore, sunburnt, wet and covered in Coke, but oh, was I happy.

Then, **new thing 11**: going bouldering. Bouldering is like rock climbing, but without a harness. Just like Spider-Man. That is, a version of Spider-Man that is—plot twist!—a suburban mum in Kmart activewear underneath the slick red suit. I'm sure the real Spider-Man looks equally as terrified under his mask as I did. Like the biking and dragon boating, bouldering pushed my body and reminded me how amazing it is. Who cares what sort of hair lotion you've used when you're concentrating on biking, rowing or climbing? Not me. All I cared about was making my body work. While bouldering, all I cared about was hanging on to the boulders, lest I fall to my doom like a Disney villain. I heard once that Disney use this because falling indicates certain death without being graphic, so is less traumatic for children. Although, technically, Scar in *The Lion King* is taken down by the hyenas after falling, but he's such a badass I'm sure nobody minds.

In the spirit of new things of a physical nature, for **new thing 12**, I joined a team for a push-up competition. This was something I needed to really train for. Push-ups are deceptive. They look so easy: you're just going up and down, after all. But push-ups are bloody hard, especially when you are a woman who is large of nork. I needed to do as many as I could in a minute. Sixty seconds. It doesn't sound like much, but time is relative. The nine minutes between pressing snooze on my alarm and it piercing my soul with its beeping a second time feels like a nanosecond. Sixty seconds of push-ups feels like an epoch. An epoch of jelly-armed pain. It was gruelling, but due to my training, combined with a cheering audience and the sweet motivational sounds of 'Eye of the Tiger', on the day I blew my previous attempts at doing push-ups out of the water. It was awesome. I felt pumped and happy and didn't even care that my arms hurt so much I could hardly feed myself afterward.

The training for the push-up competition also helped with

my next new thing, **new thing 13**: shooting a bow and arrow. The first time I tried, I missed the target. And by 'missed' I really mean 'the arrow practically went in the opposite direction before falling limply to the ground'. The old man standing beside me commented that perhaps I didn't have the muscle strength for it. I narrowed my eyes. I tried again, and hit the target right in the middle.

And how did this help my relationship with my inner voice that said I was still the third-ugliest girl?

The little voice in my head is still there sometimes. No one heals in a straight line, and putting long-held insecurities to bed takes longer than a year. I think that total closure is a myth. It's hard to unshackle yourself completely from an inner critic that has been your constant companion for over twenty years. As much as you may hate the little niggle of self-doubt, there is something comforting about its reliability and predictability. But I now know how to tell the voice to bugger off.

I'm not ugly. I never was. I was just an awkward teenager who let other people's opinions matter too much. But now I know better. I'm glad I learned so much more about style and beauty, because I enjoy it now I've calmed down about the whole thing. I know what colours suit me, and how to apply foundation and blusher without looking like an Oompa Loompa. I know that false eyelashes look fabulous, but are ultimately damaging for both my natural lashes and my wallet. I know that owning four different types of black eyeliner is never going to repair my self-esteem if I continue to lack perspective. It is true what Osip Mandelstam wrote: I'm lucky to have my body, for it works. I'm alive and I breathe, and I don't have reduced mobility or no money to buy nice clothes or have acid scars on my face. I'm lucky that the worst of my issues was bad skin, as it was something that was able to be fixed, something I throw a mental ticker-tape parade about on a near daily basis. My body is strong, and I love it for that. Others are not so fortunate. Sometimes it takes a little more body confidence to really appreciate that.

If someone voted me the third-ugliest these days, I'd walk away. Actually, no. I'd ask them to stand near that target while I hold that bow and arrow.

Because, after training for those push-ups, I'm a pretty good shot.

# 3

# COMMUNICATION,
# OLD AND NEW

❊ **New thing 14**: Doing a zip-line

❊ **New thing 15**: Going in a helicopter

❊ **New thing 16**: Detoxing from social media

❊ **New thing 17**: Handwriting a letter to a friend or family member every day for a week

❊ **New thing 18**: Starting a virtual wine and Netflix group

**THE YEAR 2005 MIGHT NOT SEEM** like that long ago, but in technological terms it's been an age. It blows my mind that during my lifetime I've witnessed a revolution with (I think) as many far-reaching implications for society as the Industrial Revolution. We all know that this change is happening around us, but most of us like our smartphones too much to philosophically deconstruct what it actually means. Plus, we're still figuring it out. We finally clue up to the fact it's annoying to send chain emails to everyone we know imploring them to forward it within seconds or else they will spontaneously combust to the tune of 'Twinkle, Twinkle, Little Star', but then technology evolves some more and it's back to square one all over again.

In 2005, the year Alan and I got together, I had a VCR player and a 14-inch TV. My camera used film, so I wouldn't see what photos looked like until a month had passed and I'd paid the pharmacist $10. More often than not the photographs weren't very flattering, but I didn't mind half as much as I do now when bad photos are taken. At least back then I could fool myself that I might have morphed into someone more photogenic in the month it took to develop the film. My parents didn't get some films developed for years. Not like now, when I can see what I look like in a photo within seconds.

Back in 2005, when I wanted to contact someone I'd pick up the phone and call. We sent text messages, but it was still a largely functional form of communication because it cost money. Emails were instant, but there were no read receipts, no little green circles telling you when someone was online, no tiny ellipsis dots telling you whether or not the person was replying at that exact moment. You didn't know how often someone checked their email, so there wasn't the same expectation of a quick reply. As you had to be physically sitting at a computer, replying was unlikely to be instant anyway. It wasn't unusual for a few days to pass before you'd hear back from someone. During that time, you had no way of knowing whether the person was ignoring you or if they were in the depths of Siberia. There was no live-time record of all of the fun things people were doing without you. In the winter of 2005 I spent a happy Saturday night in my PJs, reading the recently released *Harry Potter and the Half-Blood Prince*, and savouring every word. I didn't find out until the following Monday that some friends had hit the clubs and not invited me. If that happened now, I would know exactly what I was missing and might cry about more than Dumbledore's untimely demise. In the age of instantly uploaded photos and tags and 'check-ins', I would find out in real time and spend the evening distracted and unhappy. Instead, I snuggled into my favourite chair, listened to music on my CD player and read my book. It hurt when I did find out, sure, but it didn't ruin my weekend.

Oh, how the world has changed.

As a society, we talk so much less now. The idea of spending hours on a landline feels as archaic as sending a pigeon with a message grasped in its claws. Landline use has plummeted in recent times. In 2006, 91.6 per cent of us had access to a landline, but by 2015 that number was closer to 65 per cent,[1] a figure that is no doubt lower today. A whole generation

71

of children are being raised with no idea that 'ring ring' is the sound a phone is supposed to make. In 2005, when my landline rang I rushed towards it, wondering who it could be. I spent hours sitting at the top of the stairs chatting about my problems and catching up on gossip with people I cared about. Everyone knew the rules with landlines. You didn't call before 6 p.m, during dinner, or after 9 p.m. If someone called while you were watching the final of *Survivor*, it was fine to say, 'Can I call you back afterwards?', because the programme wasn't being recorded and was only shown once. And when someone picked up, you at least knew they were home, or else it would have gone to the answer machine. They weren't driving, or at the supermarket, or on the toilet. I don't have a landline anymore. Calling people on mobiles feels different—more serious, more official. I used to ring people all the time, some of whom I didn't even know that well. Now, I can count on one hand the number of people I'd feel comfortable calling 'just to say hi' without prearranging the time, and they are all related to me. And because people ring so rarely nowadays, when they do, you assume that it's important. So you pick up, even if you're in the middle of juggling fire on the back of a dancing elephant. I feel shy about calling friends now, even people whose childhood phone numbers I still know by heart. At some point over the past fifteen years, ringing someone for no reason started to feel like an invasion of the other person's privacy.

Smartphone ownership in Western countries varies between 71 and 90 per cent depending on the country, and Americans check their phones an average of almost 50 times a day.[2] Our phones are ever-present friends that give us instant gratification and repetitive strain injury. I get pains in my thumb and right hand if I use my mobile too often—considering average smartphone users 'tap, click and swipe' a whopping 2617 times a day, it's little wonder.[3] That's a lot of movement in our hands we weren't evolved to do and a big change from spearing woolly mammoths.

These phones aren't just pieces of technology, not anymore. They feel like extensions of us, like extra limbs. According to one study, more than half of the people surveyed would choose to give up chocolate, caffeine, alcohol or exercise for a week rather than spend a week without their mobile. Twenty-one per cent would even give up their shoes.[4] When I read that I had to have a good think about whether I'd give up my shoes or my phone for a week if it was one or the other. On one hand, my shoes keep my feet warm, social convention dictates we wear them in public, and standing on stones barefoot really hurts. On the other hand, my phone is where I listen to music, get my news and feel connected. Plus, I love pedicures, so being barefoot for a week might just be manageable, if it wasn't snowing or anything, as my feet would still look good. Tricky. I still haven't decided.

Many of us are addicted to the internet. Including me. Doing the rounds of all of my main sites was something I'd felt the need to do far too often: in the morning, during my lunch break, before I go to bed. I'd check my email, my Facebook, anywhere between two and five news sites, Reddit memes, and then whatever forum conversations I was embroiled in at that moment. It's the modern-day equivalent of walking out to the letterbox to see if the postman has come, but in a world where there are thousands of mailboxes and the mailman never rests. Spending time online releases what psychology professor Daniel J. Levitin calls 'a dollop of reward hormones' that come from the 'dumb, novelty-seeking portion of the brain'.[5] In 2016, Facebook joined drugs, sex, alcohol, sugar, love and gambling as the top addictions plugged into Google. Porn also featured—online porn, something else that's come about in the internet era.[6] The porn people are addicted to now is very different to the old magazines featuring women draped over cars—more dodgy stuff, less hair.

People who aren't on social media are treated with suspicion, unless they are super-smug about it, in which case everyone else just wants to give them a slap. The internet has also changed our lexicon: spam isn't fake ham in a tin, ghosting isn't anything supernatural,[7] and trolls aren't plastic creatures with an excess of hair. Etiquette faux pas exist that weren't a thing before, such as 'phubbing', short for phone-snubbing—ignoring the person you are with in favour of your phone, something Susan Krauss Whitbourne on *Psychology Today* calls 'a new way to make someone feel inferior'.[8] Thanks to emojis we can now talk in pictures in a manner not seen since the Egyptians used hieroglyphics. Alan and I do this all of the time, although I do recommend caution if you're using emojis to tell someone that you want them to pick up an eggplant at the supermarket— especially if it's someone you aren't in a relationship with. (Given my high-school nickname was Eggplant, for reasons that I no longer remember, I'm kinda sad that the meaning of the word has changed so much in the past ten years. I used to doodle an eggplant on all of my school books. I've really got to remember to tell Jack and Dahla that the word's meaning has changed. Otherwise, when I die at a ripe old age and they are sorting through my stuff, they might jump to all sorts of conclusions about my teenage extracurricular activities.)

The internet has changed friendship. We have lots of 'friends' online: in 2014, over half of Facebook users had more than 200 friends, and 15 per cent had over 500.[9] I have about 450 Facebook friends, at least 100 more than I had in 2014 when that study was undertaken, so I can imagine that the earlier figure is higher today as well. Both figures are much higher than 150, which is the figure anthropologist Robin Dunbar famously argued is the maximum number of people any individual can have a genuine relationship with.[10] I don't have a genuine relationship with all of my Facebook friends. A woman called Sarah added me last year, and it took two months for me to realise it was a totally different Sarah to who I thought it was. Facebook can make things weird too, because the etiquette is still evolving. If someone goes on an epic holiday and you like all their posts, is it weird to mention their holiday next time you see them? Is it weird to mention people's updates if you haven't liked them? Is it better to pretend you didn't see them at all? I have no idea. Like when I bumped into a Facebook friend in the supermarket, and the only thing I could think of to say was a comment about a post they'd put up that morning. Then I felt like a giant stalker when they said, 'Oh, you saw that', like they'd forgotten to put me on their restricted list or something. Awkward. I don't like de-friending people either, not unless I genuinely want them out of my life. I used to do it with wanton abandon after adopting a strict 'Would I stop and talk to them on the street?' test. However, due to the random twists and turns that life brings us, I can personally attest to what it's like to de-friend someone because you think you'll never see them again, and then wind up sitting beside them at a new job a few years later. Spoiler: it's embarrassing. Especially when they say, 'Didn't we used to be friends on Facebook?'

Social media can increase feelings of inadequacy. People's lives are shinier online, whether it's complete bollocks or not. And so much of it is bollocks. The top words women use to describe their husbands on social media are 'the best', 'my best friend', 'the greatest' and 'so cute'. The top words in online searches are 'gay',[11] 'a jerk', 'annoying' and 'mean'. The only word to appear in both lists was 'amazing'. The people whose lives aren't shinier are a whole different breed of annoying—the fishers. You know the ones: friends who post a litany of abstract, obscure and incomprehensible woes in a fishing expedition for replies that say, 'R U ok hun xoxoxo?' This sort of attention-seeking wasn't possible before the internet. Back in the day, if someone said, 'Why do bad things always happen to me?', you'd reply 'What things?', and the conversation would move on. If they didn't reply, they'd look like a knobber. And if they annoyed you, you'd stop hanging out with them. You wouldn't look at their fishing statuses while eating your dinner. Or perhaps even while using the toilet, unwittingly contributing to your phone carrying ten times more bacteria than a toilet seat.[12]

There's no doubt in my mind that, if you're in a certain headspace, social media makes you feel worse. While the academic jury is still out on whether social media use increases feelings of dislocation and loneliness or merely highlights such tendencies in people who already suffer from these issues, the American Academy of Pediatrics has nonetheless warned that Facebook can contribute to feeling depressed.[13] I get why. When times are tough, you don't want to hear that other people are #soblessed or #feelingloved. Someone's perfect self as presented on social media is always better-looking than your own unfiltered self. Then there are the photos. The glossy, shiny, filtered photos, posted by people who actually know how to use Photoshop, unlike me. Photos of children with clean faces, a perfect pedicure against white sand and baking that doesn't look like roadkill. Last century, Kodak started a marketing campaign associating taking photos with happiness in order to get people to do it more often.[14] It worked. Now it's like that age-old philosophical question: if a tree falls in the middle of the forest, and no one hears it, does it make a sound? If you do something memorable and no one takes a photo, did it even happen?

Documenting my year online was starting to influence my new things, and not always in a good way. For **new thing 14** I went zip-lining. A zip-line is essentially a very high and very fast flying fox, and it turned out it was one of my favourite new things. There were three photos taken of me that day that I love. In the 'before' photo, I am strapped into the harness wearing the terrified expression of someone about to catapult out of their comfort zone. The 'during' photo shows me mid-zip-line, suspended high above ground, with my arms outstretched in an excellent imitation of someone who wasn't filled with terror. In the final photo, the 'after' photo, I am grinning like I'm competing in the Smile Olympics and gunning for gold. I think of the zip-line more than any of the other new things I did around that period, and strongly suspect it's because of the photo montage. I wonder: if I didn't have my Kodak moment and a series of photos that got me lots of Facebook 'likes', would I think of it at all? Have those photos altered my memories?

**New thing 15** was my first-ever helicopter ride. The entire journey took inside of 15 minutes as we went up, circled above Wellington a few times, then came back down to ground again. For the first half of the trip, I was so busy taking photos I completely forgot to enjoy what I was doing. Then: tragedy struck! My battery died, so no more photos for me. I was desolate, and then scared as the Imp of the Scaredy-cat, my old nemesis, came back to remind me that I didn't much like being up high. Then I did something completely unusual for this day and age. I looked out the window. With my eyes. My actual eyes! Not through a wee screen. Then, because I was looking with my actual eyes, I spotted my house. It was epic. If my battery hadn't died, I'd have more photos of that helicopter ride, but fewer memories. I thought back to my failed free-fall. It's painful to admit, but if there had been someone I'd known there to watch me, I might have done it. Even more embarrassing to admit: if that person had been taking photos for me to put online, I almost certainly would have gone through with it. I'd become one of *those* people.

Detoxing from social media was something I'd been meaning to do for some time, without success. I'd always thought that there was no need to self-flagellate about my social-media habit. I reassured myself that social media activates the same part of the brain as cocaine, and is known to be addictive, so it wasn't my fault.[15] According to the Internet Addiction Test, I was only a 'mild' addict. My results read: 'You may surf the Web a bit too long at times, but you have control over your usage.' I wasn't even deemed 'moderate', let alone 'severe'. I also scored low on the Bergen Facebook Addiction Scale.[16] So, I didn't have a problem, and there were so many reasons to stay online. What if I missed important news? Facebook was how I found out about who was having babies, who had moved overseas and who was getting married. And more recently: who had died. I learned that a friend had passed away after his profile picture was changed to a photo of his headstone, six months after his death.[17] When a child I'd known lost his battle with cancer, I saw it in my newsfeed hours before anyone picked up a phone. Twitter was where I watched news unfold. And where else would I see memes and shares and other funny stuff? Of course I couldn't remove myself from social media. I was active in Facebook groups. It was how people contacted me. It was my social lifeline. And yet, a social-media detox was something that I needed to do because, quite simply, it made me anxious.

Why did social media trigger my anxiety so badly? First, when people sent me messages, I felt like I needed to reply right away, regardless of whether or not I had time. It felt rude not to, especially if they'd seen that I'd seen the message. This was bad for my mental health, bad for my parenting and bad for my favourite cooking pot, due to the time I got caught in a conversation and burnt the pasta sauce.

Second, I never quite knew when conversations were finished. Most of the time, I didn't care. Every now and then, though, I'd be having an in-depth conversation about something significant—like talking to someone about their problems—and would be sitting at my computer, fully engaged in the topic, fingers at the ready. Then, nothing. Except that sinking feeling of still being halfway through a conversation when the other person is done. I'm usually rational about this, but sometimes, especially in situations when the other person had got in touch to specifically discuss an issue, it would leave me feeling daft, used and a bit lame. I'd put my phone down or move away from the computer, but never completely relax, as the person might reignite the conversation again. I'd check my phone in case I'd missed a message and feel deflated when nothing was there on my lockscreen except the time and date.

Third, the little green dot. The one that tells you someone is online and not responding to your message. Like number two above, 99 per cent of the time I didn't care. But every now and again, being able to see that someone had read a message from me and not responded would send my anxiety into overdrive.

My decision to detox came after all three of these things came together.

I received a message from a friend with an update on a situation that I knew would have upset them. It was a friend who had form for being quite demanding when she needed support, but then disappearing whenever the good times returned. And I mean *demanding*. It wasn't unusual to get a dozen messages in a day as she sapped my energy like an emotional vampire. It was distracting and draining, not to mention frustrating. The whole dynamic made me feel like I'd slipped back into a time-space loop and I was at high school all over again. We'd been friends for so long, though, that if I didn't reply when I knew she was distressed, I felt guilty.

At the time, I was out with someone else enjoying a drink and a catch-up. I'd been feeling a little anxious all day for various reasons but had been keeping it in check. When my phone beeped twice, I saw the messages on the lockscreen. The person I was with in real life was talking, but my mind fractured in half, listening to the person who I was with but also thinking about what my other friend had sent. My phone beeped again. Another message: 'Where are you?' I tried to ignore it as I was in the middle of something else, so I put my phone on silent and in my pocket. I'd forgotten to disable the vibrate function, though, which went about twenty minutes later.

'Lauren? Are you dead?'

As soon as I got home, I booted up my computer so I could send a proper, considered response.

During our conversation, I gave her problem my full

attention. I wanted to help. I had things to say. I cared. She replied with a long blurb of information that had been cut and pasted from a conversation she was having at the same time with someone else. All that harassing me, when I wasn't even the only person she was talking to about her problems?

And then, she walked away from the conversation and left me on read, right after I had said something particularly well thought-out. I was tired and at a low ebb, so my social anxiety kicked in. Had I said the wrong thing? Was she mad at me? Rational me knew that it probably wasn't even a thing, but I wasn't rational. I had caught the anxiety bug that I had been fighting off all day and was surfing every jittery, nervous, hyper-aware wave.

Eventually, I got a response—a throwaway comment that hit one of my sensitive spots like a knife through the heart. I was so cross I couldn't see straight. All the pent-up anger about her feeling entitled to my time and attention and giving nothing in return, plus ruining my evening by constantly messaging, then sending a cut-and-paste message, then ignoring me. And now this? She should have known better than to say what she had said in the first place, and I shot back with a message that I would never have sent in the cold light of day, let alone said in person. It dripped with melodrama and absolutes and should never have left my fingers. She saw the message, but didn't respond. Ditto the messages over the following days that I saw as olive branches, but that she later described as ferocious. I imagine the truth sits somewhere in between, given how anxious it made me feel as the little green dot taunted me:

she was online, but not responding. My mind was not clear. As everyone who understands anxiety knows, the more anxious you feel, the more you need affirmation. The less affirmation you get, the more anxious you become. This was someone I was used to hearing from multiple times a day, so the lack of response was even more obvious. I was in a right spin.

This wasn't her problem, though. Or Facebook's problem. It was *my* problem, and it was time to step away.[18] Thus began one of my hardest new things to date, **new thing 16**, detoxing from social media.

Like giving up any other addiction, detoxing from social media was tough. I hadn't realised how often I checked it until I couldn't anymore—I would pick up my phone to look while standing at a checkout, waiting for the bus or sitting in bed. I'd even do it while talking to people, phubbing them by accident. I spent the first day of the detox feeling out of kilter and worrying about how many messages I was missing. I sneakily reactivated my account to check on day two, but after someone saw me online and gave me a ribbing for breaking my detox I was careful not to do that again. I became worried that something big had happened that everyone in the world knew about except me. Once, I even logged back into Facebook on autopilot, and the account reactivated itself as though I'd never been away. I swiftly logged back out, but not before I saw that I had nine unread messages in my account that would prey on my mind for the next week.

There were aspects of social media that I really missed. I'd underestimated how much Facebook was a launch pad for my other internet surfing—clicking on articles friends had 'liked', looking at memes and seeing funny shares. I missed my Facebook groups, and the sense of community I've found there. For all my angst about the conversation that had ended my friendship, I missed the other low-key banter conversations I was used to having. I didn't miss reading about the minutiae of people's lives, but I missed the real updates. I liked emailing friends, but still missed the passive perusing of updates from people I don't know well enough to send an email to. I realised that, if it weren't for Facebook, I wouldn't be in touch with these people at all.

I also missed some important things. The venue of my exercise class got moved. It was posted to the Facebook page but no one checked whether I'd got the message, and I went to the wrong place. I missed an invitation to a party from someone I didn't know well; she'd invited all of her Facebook friends and hadn't noticed I wasn't there anymore. I had no way of finding out where my book club was being hosted that month, so didn't go. I didn't have phone numbers for any of the other members; we'd all met in the last few years, so never swapped numbers. All of our contact was through WhatsApp or Messenger.

There were positive things about quitting social media cold turkey as well. I did more writing, I read more, I slept better due to less ogling of screens while sitting in bed. I would be at home and suddenly realise that I didn't know where my phone was. I felt liberated. I was a better parent, because I wasn't distracted all the time. I was less anxious and

I felt in control, for, while I had given out my email address, I would only check this when in a position to reply. And when I was feeling listless, staring into space wasn't so bad. I hadn't realised how much time I had been spending formulating status updates in my head.

I logged back on after two weeks because it was getting too hard to manage my life without all of the groups. School news, catch-ups with friends—it's all done via social media. It was nice to be back, but I had learned my lesson, and used it more mindfully. I stopped using social media when I was tired, and tried not to worry when people walked away from conversations. I also made better use of the 'mute conversation' and 'do not disturb' functions, and uninstalled some apps from my phone. I couldn't live without social media—the world has moved on too much—but detoxing for that time was an important part of me managing my use.

The effects of that time offline lasted longer than I expected. I found out months later that a friend from school had had a baby during my two-day blackout, and I'd missed it. Someone with cancer had taken a turn for the worse and it had been posted on Facebook, but I hadn't seen it. Social media is a reality of life for me—I just needed to learn to self-manage better. It's like cake. It's everywhere, but that doesn't mean you should eat lots of it every day.

For **new thing 17**, I wrote a letter, by hand, every day for a week. Before the internet took over, I used to spend hours and hours pouring out my heart and soul to friends and family scattered around the world. And was there ever a moment more delightful then opening the letterbox and recognising a dear friend's handwriting on an envelope within? Especially a dear friend I hadn't received a letter from in a while, for even my closest friends would write only once every two or three weeks, which is a lot of news to catch up on when the written word is your only form of communication. I still have these letters, as do the women who were my best friends at the time. We've agreed to swap them at some point, so we can each read what we wrote when our teenage angst was at full throttle. I'm not sure I want to yet. I'm not ready to cringe that much. With all due respect to my teenage self, she could be a real earnest, pretentious, egocentric dickhead sometimes.

My collection of letters remains one of my most valuable possessions, especially those from people who have passed. When I first left home, my elderly great aunt wrote to me at least once a month—long letters about the weather and her garden and who she had lunch with. In among the seemingly inconsequential details of her life there would also be some nuggets of advice. 'Travel broadens the mind,' she wrote in her last letter to me. 'You are wise to embrace it. I hope you'll be able to come and visit the next time you are home.' I never did get to visit; she had a stroke the following month and died not long afterward. And yet . . . She may have been gone for twenty years, but part of her essence lives on in those letters—

her handwriting, her turn of phrase. The blue floral paper with matching envelopes she thought nice enough to spend her pension on. Her name, written in her own hand. A screen grab of an instant-messenger conversation just isn't the same. What stays in the corner but travels all around the world? A stamp. Jack got this joke in a Christmas cracker recently but had no idea what it was about—he'd never heard of a postage stamp. And why would he have?

For my letter-writing challenge, I started by writing to the same people I wrote to as a teenager. I then wrote to my dad, and to my children. I wrote to other friends scattered around the world. Then, channelling my inner earnest, pretentious, egocentric dickhead self, I wrote a letter to me of the future. It turns out that my handwriting is even less legible than before, and since when did writing hurt my hand so much? My pinky was raw from rubbing on the paper and the muscles in my hand ached—poor muscles that had barely been used for years. I'd recently read that Cambridge University was considering allowing laptops in exams,[19] and tut-tutted like the Luddite I believed myself to be. *What is the world coming to?* I thought. *How can the sacred art of handwriting be lost?* After my week of writing letters, I had more sympathy. I'd forgotten that typing on a computer was much faster than writing by hand, and typing had never given me a callus on my finger. Plus, I missed emojis. Not the giant thumb, mind you. My hatred of the giant thumb could fill a whole other book. The other ones: Mr Smiley, Mr Winky, the wine glasses and the grinning face, the devil face and the biceps. I wrote 'lol' in my letters, and wondered how on earth I told jokes back in the day without the laughing-with-tears emoji. I probably didn't tell jokes at all, I concluded. I was probably too busy being earnest, pretentious and egocentric. Teenage me didn't need emojis, unless there is a 'wearing too much black and writing bad poetry' emoji. Teenage me didn't know what she was missing out on in many respects.

I found while writing letters that focusing on one thing at a time was embarrassingly difficult. There is no flicking between browser windows when all you have is paper. It seems my attention span shrank about the same time my hand muscles weakened. But focusing on this one thing meant that the people I wrote to were in my head the whole time. I wasn't having multiple conversations at once while sitting on the bus. This made me feel closer to the people I was writing to, which made me miss them. Writing letters is more intimate than writing messages, so I felt braver about telling them how I felt. I wrote 'I miss you', 'I can't wait to see you again', 'Love you'. Writing made me feel less lonely. Even though I was completely alone at the time of writing, the act of doing so reminded me that these lovely people were in the world. We may not speak all the time, but they are still out there for me, as I am them.

The people I wrote to got in touch. You made my day, one said. Two tagged me in posts about how happy the letters had made them. Two wrote back. It felt good to have brought a sliver of joy into the lives of the people I cared about. Writing to faraway friends has since become one of the things I do when I feel the cold slap of loneliness encroaching. I don't write letters—it was a good experiment, but getting to the post shop to send them was a pain in the bum. I do write longer messages or emails, though—messages that aren't dependent on a reply. The very act of writing makes me feel connected, and puts these people in my head in a way that reminds me that they are far away, but they are still there. I may not see them often, or talk often, but they are only the press of a button away.

The things I'd missed during my social-media detox gave me ideas for ways to feel less lonely. There is so much opportunity online if you take it. I started actively participating in a local online group of brilliant and amazing women, putting on my brave face and turning up to events where I didn't know a soul. Through this online group, I went to real-life dinners and clothes swaps, to plays and to a ball. It turns out one of the women lives around the corner. I introduced her to another friend one evening.

'We met online,' I said.

'Huh,' said the friend I'd met via more conventional methods. 'I thought that was just dating.'

'It's okay,' my new-buddy-from-the-internet said, 'I'm not a serial killer.'

Further channelling what is good about the internet, for **new thing 18** I started a virtual wine and Netflix group as well as one that met in real life. The virtual group was a bigger success, and it didn't take long until there were a number of members I've never met before—friends of friends—or others I didn't know well beforehand. I love that wee group. We talk about the television we've watched, swapping views and theories and recommendations. As a society we live in the golden age of television. Gone are the days of having nothing else to watch on Saturday night apart from a movie I've seen four years earlier and didn't even really like the first time around. But there is so much choice, it's overwhelming. It helps having a space to talk about it. I'm often at home alone, and the cold hand of loneliness lurks in my peripheral vision. This is when I turn to the group and see what shows have been recommended. Or I ask, 'I want something trashy but good, any recommendations?' Or 'Any ideas for something serious and intense?' The responses come right away. I then watch the show alone in my living room, but I'm not lonely. I'm part of a community that's based in my mobile phone.

So what of my friend who triggered my social media detox?

One weekend, she had a birthday party. I wasn't invited. I hadn't expected to be invited, for we hadn't spoken in some time, but my other friends had been. In the days beforehand I was asked by mutual friends: 'Will you be there?', 'See you at the party?', 'Hope to see you on Saturday?' Each time, I felt sad—I had lost my friend, and now I felt ostracised as well. I also felt uncomfortable; I didn't want to lie about being busy when I wasn't, but I didn't want to burden our mutual friends with drama. The day of the party, I spent the evening thinking about what my alternate-version self would be doing. I'd be heading into town instead of being at home wearing my yoga trousers and grey polar fleece. I'd be having a few quiet drinks and a bit of banter, not just with her, but other friends as well.

The evening of the party I felt lonely, and it was made all the worse by social media. She put a photo of the party up on Facebook at 10 p.m., her first post in over two years, and tagged a mutual Facebook friend so it showed up in my feed. I could see, in real time, what I was missing, and it sucked. The loneliness hit me in the face. So I opened my computer and wrote a long email to my friend in Denmark. I chatted to my mum on Messenger, my dad via a series of emoji-laden text messages, and then settled in to watch a show that the virtual wine and Netflix group had recommended. I remembered that this former friend wasn't particularly nice anyway, and that she'd used me for years. I remembered that even if I had gone to the party, I may not have enjoyed it. I realised that having been friends with someone for a long time is no reason to continue if they don't treat you well. Then I thought, *This is fine. This version of me is the one I want to be.* For all of the bad things about the internet, it's that sense of connection over time and place that makes modern technology something to be valued.

Even if we never see a person's handwriting anymore.

# 4

# LOVE, MARRIAGE, HORSE, NO CARRIAGE

❄ **New thing 19**: Doing couple counselling

❄ **New thing 20**: Swimming with sharks

❄ **New thing 21**: Feeding lions

❄ **New thing 22**: Doing a night
tour of a wildlife sanctuary

❄ **New thing 23**: Getting my tarot cards read

❄ **New thing 24**: Riding a horse

### I'D ALWAYS WANTED TO GET MARRIED.

Of all the parts of the script, getting married was the scene I wanted the most. Of all life's variables, it was also the one thing that I assumed would definitely happen. It wasn't a case of 'if', it was a matter of 'who' and 'when'.

When I was a little girl, my sisters and I used to play 'weddings'. We took it in turns to prance around in Mum's old wedding dress, while the others swayed, doe-eyed, to terrible music. At the age of ten, I asked Mum what the happiest day of her life was. She said she didn't know. I was confused. How could the answer be anything other than her wedding? At thirteen, I wrote in my diary what I wanted my future husband to be like. He had to be handsome, I said. He had to be musical. Most importantly, I wrote, he had to have 'done IT' before, for I would most certainly be a virgin, and wouldn't know what to do on my wedding night. Not 'it'; thirteen-year-old me was clear on that point. IT. My thirteen-year-old self would have been shocked at the version of me that got married . . . Let's just say Alan isn't musical and leave it at that.

I loved movies with happy endings: romantic comedies and sweeping love stories. The part in *Titanic* that made me cry the hardest was the touching scene with the elderly couple cuddling in bed. When I was single at 24, someone at work was playing with a Magic 8-Ball. 'Will Lauren be married in the next two years?' she asked, shaking the ball. 'Yes' the ball said, and I wished upon wish that it would be true. I'd decided on the song I'd walk up the aisle to long before I had anyone to meet me at the other end, and I told my sisters that they would one day be my bridesmaids. They upset me once. (I can't remember why. I think it was linked to one sister's poor financial regulation when performing the sacred duty of Monopoly banker.) 'You'll never be my bridesmaids,' I said to them. At the time, I couldn't think of anything more cutting to say. That's how important my theoretical, non-existent future marriage was to me, even though I was single at the time.

There were a few frogs to be kissed first, but I was always sure I'd find my prince and have my happily ever after. That was the way things worked, after all. It was implicit in all the self-help breakup manuals my friends and I quoted at each other. It was explicit in our favourite such book, the single girl's Bible, *He's Just Not That Into You*. We shouldn't waste time on the losers who aren't that into us, the book says, for 'there's a guy out there who wants to marry you'.[1] Those words brought me comfort after a date went badly, or when someone I felt a spark with turned out to be a bit off. Like the charming young man who told me he liked to masturbate and cry, or the fine gent who said I made him so nervous he would do bourbon shots before we hung out— even if we were meeting in the morning. Indeed, I was sure that I'd meet my soulmate. It was just a matter of time.

The human need for partnership is hardwired in our genes.[2] It's something most people want. I read one survey of a bunch of seventeen- and eighteen-year-old girls in which almost

85 per cent said marriage was 'extremely important'. Seventy-seven per cent of boys that age felt the same.[3] In another survey of university students, almost three quarters of respondents said they'd sacrifice their other life goals for romance.[4] That's a disturbing thought. Almost three-quarters of these university students were prepared to make decisions that might affect their entire lives based on having been seduced by the stories of happily ever after.

Indeed, getting married is something most of us expect we'll do—if not get married, find a person to have a significant and serious relationship with. It's one of those things that doesn't even feel like a conscious choice when you're young. It's simply part of the script most people expect their lives to follow. Marriage is also something most of us are pretty clueless about at the point we're making the decision to do it. Many people marry relatively young, at least for the first time. I was 27. Apparently that's about the time many women marry, with 29 being the tipping point where more women are married than not. The same age for men is 30.[5] It's an age when many people still don't have a clear idea of what they want to do with their lives, what career they want and what they want to define themselves by. It's also an age when many people haven't had that much relationship experience, certainly not with long-term relationships. There hasn't been enough time. We are still growing and changing, a journey that lasts our entire lives. When you're 27, all you can do is hope that you and the person you've married grow and change in parallel, like two sides of a train track. At that age you can never know for sure; you just have to commit to trying your very hardest. Then all that's left is to hope that you get it right and that your two sides of the train track don't end up shooting off in different directions.

The best way to ensure that the railway tracks keep going in the same direction is to have solid foundations. But we don't grow up watching movies about would-be lovers who have long conversations about their financial priorities before riding off into the sunset. The movies and books don't show you what happens after the big romantic kiss or the final scene. We don't see Cinderella asking her prince to please not trim his toenails in bed, or Snow White wishing she was back with the seven dwarves after her prince turned out to be a sex pest. We don't see the prince feeling disappointed that, after five years together, Rapunzel let down her hair in all regions. We don't see the low-level niggles about who is putting out the recycling, who is spending too much time on the Xbox, or whether or not one partner needs to be more diligent at hanging up the bath mat.

When most people think about love, it's the giddy love that they think about—the spark, the love at first sight. It's the addictive dopamine fix.[6] It's what psychologist Shauna H. Springer calls the 'cocaine rush' stage of relationships, which is 'based on the mutual fantasy that you and the other person are ideally matched and perfectly suited for each other'.[7] It's the love Aristotle wrote about when he said, 'Love is composed of a single soul inhabiting two bodies'.[8] It's during this phase that we go gaga about someone, and if they tick enough boxes we leap to a bunch of conclusions about their character and values being aligned with our own. Being this mentally addled means we risk projecting on to the other person who we want them to be and ignoring evidence about who they actually are, because we *want* them to be the other half of our fractured soul. It's that fun and giddy time when you try new things and embrace their hobbies and interests with gusto because you're desperate to know more about this fabulous being. It's why I read all of the Game of Thrones books and Alan watched two seasons of *Desperate Housewives*. It's when you do things, in the words of a friend who watched a Harry Potter movie on a third date even though he knew he wasn't a fan, 'to show I care about her interests, and all that shiz'.

But this is flawed. Chemical 'love' generally doesn't last longer than eighteen months to two years. It can't last forever, especially that initial lovey-dovey phase. No one would get any work done otherwise. We'd never get any sleep either, because we'd be too busy shagging and staying up all hours talking about how fabulous we both are. That's about the point that the transition from being 'in love' to 'love' happens, the transition Louis de Bernières wrote about in *Captain Corelli's Mandolin* when he said, 'love is a temporary madness' but '[t]hat is just being "in love", which any fool can do. Love itself is what is left over when being in love has burned away.'[9] I imagine this is why many relationships end at this point, because you have seen each other for the people you actually are, not who you want each other to be. If you've put the other person on a pedestal and they've fallen off, you might feel betrayed or tricked. You might say to the other person: 'you've changed'; 'you've let yourself go'; 'I thought I knew you'. But the other person is just being themselves. They might, finally, feel secure enough to wear comfortable underwear rather than lacy numbers that look like dental floss. They might feel safe enough in the relationship to abandon all of the dating advice about 'treating 'em mean to keep 'em keen' or 'making him work for it', revealing their true and vulnerable self to an emotionally avoidant person who's only been attracted to them in the first place because they liked the thrill of the chase. They might let the nice-person mask finally slip, revealing the arsehole concealed underneath. Or the couple might find that the only thing they really had in common was an all-consuming desire to bonk like rabbits.

Once the lust or giddy 'in love' is gone, if there isn't a strong foundation of friendship, mutual respect and shared values, the wheels start to fall off the good-times wagon. To get past this point, people need more than mutual attraction and dopamine to keep things going. You need what Aristotle called 'complete friendship' between two people who are 'alike in their virtue'.[10] Or, at the very least, to have a similar outlook on life. To 'have and to hold for as long as we both shall live' is a long time to disagree with someone about religion, politics, the environment, basic parenting philosophy and how often it's acceptable to get takeaways for dinner. It's a long time to spend with someone who doesn't make you laugh, or can't give you emotional support when you need it.

There are other factors at play, too. One is the 'honeymoon-as-ceiling effect': the theory that the quality of a marriage very rarely increases after the wedding day.[11] I don't agree with this. If I were to analyse my own marriage, I'd probably put my peak happiness at about our fifth anniversary. It does remind me of something someone told me once, though. Imagine if every time you had a meaningful conversation with your partner during the first year of your relationship, a jellybean was put in a jar. Then, imagine that, after one year, you took a jellybean out each time such a conversation occurred. I was told that in most relationships, no matter the length, the jar would never get empty. This I believe. There are only so many times that you can tell the stories of when you were young. Sleep becomes more important than lying in bed talking. Flirty banter turns into one-word messages: Milk! Bread! Nappies! In long-term relationships, it's easy to take the other person for granted. When I talk to my girlfriends, there are so many common themes in their relationship issues: they feel ignored; their partner is lovely as pie to colleagues all day but grumpy at home; they have disagreements about parenting; one or the other person spends too much time looking at a screen of some description; there is resentment at carrying the mental load; there are mismatched libidos. It's like bad-relationship bingo.

When kids are part of the equation, it becomes even harder to nurture your relationship. Sleep is a finite resource, like water in the desert. When you're so tired you're barely functional, it takes a lot of love and empathy to say to your partner, 'You stay in bed. I'll get up.' When you're tired, the gift of sleep is much harder to give than flowers and chocolates and all of the other declarations of love that we're told are the hallmarks of true love. Instead, it's too easy to slip into the martyr game, where you list all of the things you have done for the household and expect a giant shiny medal in the form of an extra hour in bed. Plus, now you have kids, there are people in the world who you (should) love more than your partner. At some point you stop looking for things you have in common, and start to disagree more robustly about things you don't see eye to eye on. Alan and I bonded over a love of movies. Years later, one of the biggest arguments we'd ever have was about whether or not *The Hurt Locker* was worthy of an Oscar. Somewhere along the line we'd grown apart and it had all gone wrong. It wasn't the script I'd wanted at all.

Even though separation and divorce is a statistical reality for so many who get married, there's no script for when you do. Advice on *getting* married is everywhere. There are magazines you can buy and online forums to read. On the subject of weddings and marriage (for, to many people, they are one and the same), it seems everyone has something to say: who should pay for a hen's night, whether guests can wear white to the wedding; the etiquette for inviting children; who should pay for the alcohol; whether or not a bridesmaid ought to be sacked for dying her hair bright blue. Not so with separation. People don't know how to react. Especially if nothing bad has happened.

When Alan and I first separated, I was asked if he had ever hit me. No. Someone asked whether one of us had been 'sleazy'. Again, no. What about financial problems? According to finance expert Mary Holm, Relationship Services has reported that differing views on finances is the most common reason for relationships ending.[12] That makes sense. How you spend your money (or not) is the tip of an iceberg, sitting above your values, ideologies and desires. Everyone's a bit different when it comes to what's more important: packing your lunch and saving money, or paying to sleep in that bit longer in the morning and buy it? Spending money on objects or experiences? Buying your child's birthday cake to free up time? Or staying up until midnight the night before, trying to get the chocolate dinosaur spikes just right, then getting cross and eating the spikes, thus necessitating a swift change from a stegosaurus to a long neck, but still being pleased you saved money? Not to mention your innate ability or inability to resist instant gratification and plan for the future.[13] Everyone's a bit different, so it's little wonder so many couples fight about money. Especially if they don't have much and lurch from payday to payday. But was this a problem for Alan and me? No, not really. Apart from one dark day in which the need for a four-slice toaster was debated at length and with much vigour, we'd always been on much the same page with finances. Four-slice-toaster-gate was no *Hurt Locker*. For us, separation was nothing like that—nothing so black and white. It was simple and complicated all at once, in that the thing that made Alan and me Alan and me was gone, and we didn't know how to get it back.

Of course, the question of why it happened is one I've asked myself a lot. A chronic over-thinker at the best of times, this is something that literally kept me up at night. Ruminating too much is like chewing gum once the flavour has gone, pulling it out of your mouth and putting it back in its wrapper, then later putting it back in your mouth and being surprised that it tastes exactly the same. You get to a point where it doesn't even help to think about a thing, because the truth feels more muddled every time you do. To paraphrase the musical group Keane, you'll end up digging for a truth that can't be found.[14] I mentioned earlier about the jellybeans in the jar; if I'd eaten a jellybean every time I asked myself where things went wrong with Alan, I'd be the size of Saturn and without any teeth. My excessive and sometimes obsessive rumination led to a few conclusions that whirled around in my mind until felt half-crazed.

After having children, Alan and I started socialising apart, because going out together was impossible without babysitters. Of course, if we had a magic time-machine and could go back, we would have used babystitters more. My aunt, mum and sisters have been fabulous babysitters over the years, but at that time we'd used them so much for things that really mattered that it felt like taking the piss to ask them to sit so we could go to the pub for a burger. And we didn't pay anyone to do it either, for a mixture of financial reasons and pure inertia. Now we have the benefit of hindsight, Alan and I are wise in such matters, as those with the benefit of hindsight so often are. If you can afford babysitters, they are so worth the money. Time out alone is like getting your teeth checked: it allows you to cut problems off at the pass before small holes turn into root canals. If you have sitters, you get to do things together that involve not wearing at-home clothes, things that are fun and nice and give you a window into each other's lives outside of family life. If money is tight, you can make arrangements with other people to babysit each other's kids, such as alternating fortnights, which is a win for everyone concerned. Especially if the other person has angel children who sleep more than your own children, thus giving you relaxing evenings in front of someone else's television without your own household chores taunting you. Indeed, when it comes to babysitting, there are options. I didn't realise it at the time, though, so we did very little together. Alan and I had both made new friends, me through work and parenting groups, and him through his hobbies. We didn't know each other's friends anymore. You can be different versions of yourself with different people, and the version of me I was with the friends I'd made in recent years was different from the person I was with Alan. I think I liked my friend-version more than my Alan-version. Not because of Alan, but because the version of me Alan saw had so much housework to do and slouched around the house in old, stained clothes.

We had a party not long before our separation, a housewarming with so many guests you could hardly move. It was an amazing evening—I laughed and chatted and went into town afterward and danced the night away. I didn't notice anything amiss until someone pointed out to me later that it felt very much like my friends and Alan's friends were in separate groups. Because my new friends didn't really know Alan, as soon as we hit troubled waters and I started talking to the people around me about it, I was talking to people who weren't what Shirley Glass calls 'friends of the marriage'.[15] Not because they were arseholes who wanted us to separate. It was simply that they didn't know Alan so couldn't call my bullshit if I lost perspective about the state of our relationship or who Alan and I were as people.

This compounded the other issue we had: the good old-fashioned parenting-killing-the-romance gig. When you've got kids, however hard you and your partner try to be on the same team, there are times when you're running towards separate goals. Not only are the chores endless, but you end up having to constantly negotiate with each other. Who gets to lie in? Who will get up to clean the urine-soaked sheets at 3 a.m.? Whose invitation to a Great Fun Event on a Saturday evening is more important, and who will have to stay at home? Who will call in sick to look after a child when the vomiting bug of doom comes knocking? This last one is particularly difficult, because it requires a conversation with a hidden subtext. Who is busier at work? Whose job is more important? Who earns more? At this moment in time, whose career comes first?

In all my tossing and turning and putting the chewing gum in and out of my mouth, though, I decided that our separation was about how we had changed as people, and how our 2017 versions weren't as well matched as our 2005 versions had been. The dynamic we shared when we were twenty-somethings didn't work as well in our late thirties. We had both changed. Motherhood grounded me. I discovered writing—a hobby very solitary by nature and difficult to share. Alan had always needed cave time but, whenever he stepped out of his cave, I'd be there, waiting. When I became more introverted, he'd step out of his cave, but I wouldn't be there like I used to be. I'd be in my own cave. And when I decided to come out of mine, he'd be back in his. We didn't realise this was a problem until it was too late. We didn't realise that we needed some sort of phone line between our two caves until weeks would pass and we hadn't had a single conversation that wasn't about groceries, the children or chores. We'd both changed individually, so the definition of who we were together had also changed. By simply growing up and flourishing as individuals, our railway tracks had started to veer in opposite directions.

I wanted to do new things with Alan and to get us back on track. I'd been planning on completing my first new thing, doing a confidence course through the treetops at Adrenalin Forest, alone. But having Alan climbing through the treetops with me that sunny Saturday afternoon reminded me of what we risked losing if we didn't give things another go. We weren't quite ready yet, though. I had to park my hurt; we had more work to do. So, for **new thing 19**, we went to couple counselling.

I knew my body language was textbook hostile during our first session. I couldn't help it. You can know that something's a good idea in theory but still hate it, and the first counselling session was about as fun as putting nails through one's eyelids.

Especially having to tell a complete stranger why we were there, with Alan and I tripping over each other to explain our different narratives about how we got from A to B, stopping every now and again to glare at each other. Turns out the story I was telling myself didn't stand up to external scrutiny and was very different to what Alan thought about things.

This came as a surprise: I'd told my story many times, I just hadn't told it to Alan. He said I'd never told him about how I felt the year before we separated. Hadn't I? I thought I had, but maybe I hadn't. After the first session I thought back to all the moments I felt sad, but couldn't remember a single time I'd actually said it to him with conviction. I'd tried, but backed down when the conversations got hard. There was always a good reason to not talk about it: I was tired; the kids needed something; there was work to do. I felt defensive. It wasn't my fault. It was Alan's fault for not being able to read my mind. It was Alan's fault for not embracing the new version of me that I quite liked being. It was Alan's fault for acting like a dick. (It says something about what a good person Alan is that, even then, the worst I ever thought of him was that he was a bit of a dick.) It was Alan's fault for explicitly saying to the counsellor that he really wanted us to work, and me knowing that I wanted us to work as well, but him not being able to magically make all the hurt go away. If that wasn't proof Alan was a dick, what was? That was my completely unemotional, rational assessment of the situation at that time, anyway. I wasn't being childish at all . . . no, not a bit. I wasn't being a bit of a dick, either. No, of course I wasn't.

After the first session, I stalked out of the room wearing an expression that would scare small children. If I were a cartoon character there would have been a black cloud over my head. If there were a thought bubble coming from my head, it would have read something like this: @#$% #&%*@ $%*! Brené Brown writes that shame is the one emotion that overrides all others.[16] Shame makes us do stupid things and overreact to situations. That's why I yelled at Jack for chanting 'Uranus, Uranus' in the supermarket, even though he claimed afterward that he was, apparently, 'only talking about the planet'. I realise now I only yelled because a senior colleague saw us and gave me a look of disgust. I only yelled because I was embarrassed, and shame overrides all other feelings. This was true for the counselling as well. I was angry after our first session—unusually so, the shame manifested itself in this way. Stupid Alan with his stupid different narrative that was different to my *totally* accurate and unbiased own one. Stupid counsellor with his wise words that hit the mark like a truth-bullet laced in cyanide. Stupid winter for being so cold. Stupid stupid stupid. But the seeds were sown. We decided to give things another go. So we did, with the counsellor providing ongoing advice and support for the following months. Needless to say, my attitude improved after that first session. I imagine the counsellor would have refused to see us again otherwise.

According to one famous study in experimental psychology, being in situations that scare the bejeezus out of you can heighten your feelings of sexual attraction for potential partners.[17] This got my brain cogs whirring. Alan and I could do new things together that scared us! And what better way to get the fear-juices flowing than swimming with some mean-eyed killing machines? So, for **new thing 20**, we swam with sharks. Before we hopped in the tank, I asked the instructor if it was safe.

He gave me a look like he was trying not to roll his eyes. 'They're sharks,' he said. 'You signed the waiver, right?'

I was terrified. Those sharks had the coldest eyes I have ever seen up close. They have been perfectly conditioned through hundreds of millions of years of evolution to be efficient killing machines, after all. Was the shared experience of quivering with fear what brought Alan and me back together? No. But I was pleased he was there, nonetheless. Not because of adrenalin-induced 'phwoar' thoughts, but because it was comforting to have him nearby when all I could think of was *Jaws*.

Okay, so the sharks didn't work. What next? Lions! Lions met the scary criteria, so for **new thing 21**, Alan and I took a day off work for his birthday and fed lions together. It was as terrifying as the sharks. Alan was brave enough to let them lick his hand. I, on the other hand, got so frightened I dropped the meat on the wrong side of the cage. The lioness's displeased growl still haunts my dreams.

'They really are killers, aren't they?' Alan said.

I looked at the lioness's teeth and shuddered. These weren't the kind of lions that sing 'Hakuna Matata' with a friendly yet flatulent warthog. These were the kind of lions that would, if given half a chance, eat me before I could say, 'I really would taste better with salt.' Feeding lions was a fantastic experience I don't regret, but thoughts of being mauled by the King of the Beasts didn't exactly make me gag for sexy-time. Maybe scary things were overrated. It was time for something more sedate.

For **new thing 22**, we went on a night tour of Zealandia wildlife sanctuary together, something we'd been talking about doing for the past six years. Six whole years! I knew it was six years because I'd bought Alan a voucher for Christmas when Jack was three months old. The voucher had expired, unused. When Jack and Dahla were small, arranging babysitters was on the long list of Things That Are Too Hard. But—we went. Finally. It was a lovely evening together, made all the more special by the fact that we had finally made it happen. That, and me not being scared of getting eaten. We snuck away from the rest of the group and saw a kiwi scuttling through the undergrowth. It wasn't as dramatic as swimming with sharks or feeding lions, but much more special. An actual kiwi in its natural habitat! I'd never seen one outside of captivity before. I looked at Alan through my night-vision goggles, and thought: *This is neat, and I wouldn't want to be here with anyone else.*

But, was it working? Was it enough to get us back on track?

We were kind to each other, going to great lengths to avoid difficult conversations. There had been so many over the winter that neither of us wanted to talk about the big stuff anymore. At first, there was a certain comfort in discussing minutiae in a cordial way again. What should we have for dinner? I'm going to put on a delicate wash; do you want to add your shirts? I'm swinging by the supermarket; do you need anything? At first, it was nice to have my life back, to no longer worry about finances, and to be living the usual married-with-children script I'd always wanted. There was still something missing, though.

Alan is not a needy man. His personal resilience and maturity are his greatest strengths. He doesn't demand attention—never has. He's the sort of man who will be sick, changing jobs and losing a close family member to cancer, but still apologise for inconveniencing other people. I, on the other hand, usually gravitate towards people who have some sort of hurt; it's something I used to think was a good quality but now realise is something that I need to manage very carefully or else I risk living my life pandering to drama queens and people who will always see the cup as half empty. We don't have an infinite capacity for other people's problems; if someone talks to you regularly about their issues, it inevitably squeezes out someone else. It's important to be there for others, but you must always be aware of the cost if it hits a certain intensity. This speaks to Dunbar's number, which I explore further in my chapter on loneliness on page 75—the five, fifteen and 150 meaningful connections that we have capacity for, each number coming at the expense of someone else. I was so busy hearing other people's problems, I had no space left for Alan.

Like so many other people, I like offering support and help to the people around me. This is fine most of the time. It's important to be there for my friends, as most of them would be for me. In her seminal work on intense friendships and emotional affairs, Shirley Glass writes that listening too much to another person's calamities is a well-trodden path towards becoming too emotionally involved.[18] She's right. It's good to support those who matter, but there is still a time and a place for that support, as well as a limit to the support one person can give. One evening, I went out for dinner with a close friend and a number of others I barely knew. I had a lovely time, but must have been wearing my super-empathetic face as the conversations I had with these people I barely knew included one man telling me about his depression, a woman telling me about her postnatal anxiety, and hearing a long story from a third person about their dog that had its eye removed. When I got home, Alan wanted to talk about something that was worrying him. But I didn't have it in me to have a deep conversation. I was all talked out. I tried to listen properly, but the quality of my counsel was piss-poor. I'd wasted all my emotional energy on near strangers and a one-eyed dog.

Then, for **new thing 23**, I got my tarot cards read by a woman claiming to be an oracle, and my relationship with Alan improved even more.

Do you believe in oracles? Many people do. Humans have always been attracted to such things to help us understand the world around us or make decisions. The human brain is wired to see patterns, whether they exist or not. It's called apophenia: the belief that things are part of something bigger than the thing itself; part of a grander plan. When you believe in and remember such things, confirmation bias is often at play as well, so we remember the coincidences but not the times that no coincidence was to be found.[19] This is why I noticed that, when I started writing the section about my visit to the oracle, the word count of this book was 66,600. That's why, even though I had just read all about apophenia, I still couldn't shake a creepy feeling about the coincidence.

Superstitions have been around as long as we have, and usually make no sense on a rational level. But if you've been taught about them from a young age, it still feels icky and wrong to open an umbrella inside, not say 'touch wood' or to walk under a ladder. My great-aunt, the one who wrote me letters, had a button on a string. She would hold it over things and see whether it spun in a circle or swayed like a pendulum. One way meant the thing was good, the other meant the thing was bad. I have her button. It's a shame I can't remember which way means what, so it's no use to me. Maybe I should dangle the button over some arsenic to check how it reacts. Or one of the many Coke Zeros I drink, although I'd prefer to bury my head in the sand about that particular addiction. Apparently it was something she'd learned from her mother and her mother's mother before her. Other families and cultures have other traditions and beliefs; things that seem absurd from the outside but are part of the natural order of things if they've been part of your upbringing.

Understanding of and trust in science is a relatively modern phenomenon in the scheme of human history. It's only really since the Enlightenment that we have, as the name suggests, been thus enlightened. And, even now, trust in science is patchy. Something can be studied again and again and the results published in credible, peer-reviewed journals, but some people still don't believe it to be true if their intuition or their neighbour's cousin or the lady who does their hair tells them otherwise.[20] Just take a trawl through any online forum where people debate vaccinations or climate change or the Mandela effect. Actually, don't look up the Mandela effect. It's the idea that some people slip into different time–space continuums, and I lost an entire evening foraging around the corners of the internet trying to wrap my head around that one. It's this pursuit of answers and higher understanding that means so many people are interested in the spiritual world, whether it be horoscopes, palm reading or Wicca. Or, in my case, tarot cards, read by a psychic who claimed to be the oracle. I was dubious about tarot. I wasn't expecting to learn anything useful. But it was the year of new things, after all. Why not give it a whirl?

The oracle was an older woman with piercing blue eyes who did readings in a dark tent at a fair. I walked past the tent, then doubled back, curious. The smell of incense wafted out; it was just what you'd expect an oracle's tent to look like. I stepped in and sat down. I was particularly tired that day. I wasn't wearing make-up, and was rocking the bald-eyelash look caused by the fake eyelashes. To make matters worse, I had an epic coldsore in the corner of my mouth. If the zombie apocalypse had happened that day, the zombies would have thought I was already one of their undead brethren. It would have been a most excellent and cunning disguise to avoid certain zombie death.

The oracle studied the cards then fixed her blue eyes on me.

'You're run down,' she said. 'You need some rest.'

*Duh*, I thought.

'I know,' I said. 'I do.'

'No, you really do,' she said urgently. 'You're facing burnout. You need to be more bored, give things a rest. You will have success in your future, but not if you don't get rest. Be bored. Slow down. Take more care of yourself, or the good things in your future will not come to pass.'

I studied my hands. Tapping into the spiritual world or not, she was right. A warm glow spread over my body; I felt good. It was refreshing to be bossed around and told to rest. I couldn't remember the last time someone had said that to me. I *did* need to rest; my epic coldsore and depleted lashes were proof of that. I smiled, enjoying myself. I also liked being told I needed a period of doing sweet fuck-all that would then be followed by untold joy and happiness. Sitting in that tent, I didn't even care that it could all have been bollocks. It felt like counselling, but with more optimism and less awkward self-reflection. This was so much easier to digest.

The oracle then talked me through other predictions, some of which have since come true and some not, before looking back up at me.

'Do you have a specific question for the cards?' the oracle asked.

'I want to ask about the future of my relationship,' I said.

I drew some more cards, and in the future position sat the card of Death. I studied the card on the table in front of me. It's a creepy-looking mofo. Even if it didn't say 'death' you'd still know it didn't mean goodness and light, unlike the nice cards with happy-looking people holding cups. Uh-oh.

'It doesn't mean your relationship will end,' the oracle said quickly. 'I think it means that whatever has held you back is now dead.'

I felt for her. Explaining the death card to panicked clients must be a real occupational hazard in oracle circles.

'Or,' she said, 'it means your relationship will be dead if you don't make the right changes.'

'Ah,' I said. 'Sure. Thanks.'

I looked at the card again and realised how much I wanted my marriage to work. I narrowed my eyes. *No death on my watch*, I thought. *No way.*

Ever done that thing when you can't make a decision so you flip a coin? Then, when the coin lands on heads, you think: *No! I didn't want it to be heads!* Alan and I did this once with ice creams. One was mint and one was boysenberry. Neither of us minded which one we ate, so we flipped a coin. But when the coin told me I'd be eating the boysenberry, I thought: *No! I want mint!* Tarot was like this for me, but instead of ice cream, it was relationships. Since my tarot reading I've done more research about it. For many who use tarot, it's not so much about telling the future as it is providing a snapshot of your life right now. Or, to quote from *The Tarot Bible*, tarot 'provides a mirror image of ourselves and the moment we choose to look at our reflection'.[21] I'd say looking at that death card was like looking at my reflection, but I'm not that skeletal. Nonetheless, I'd flipped that coin, and I knew what I wanted. It wasn't the boysenberry ice cream or another separation. It was the mint ice cream. It was being with Alan, and the death card meaning just what the oracle said it would. And that alone, made the visit to the oracle worthwhile, whether you believe in such things or not.

For **new thing 24**, Alan thought hard about things I'd never done before, and took me horse riding for our anniversary. It was our eleventh anniversary. Eleven years! It's not that long when you consider that humans have only walked the Earth for 0.0001 per cent of its history.[22] But then it feels like a very long time when I think that when I first got together with Alan I'd never heard of social media, gay people couldn't get married and I thought that *Sex and the City* was feminism at its best. How times have changed.

Like many couples, we used to do special things for our anniversary. We fulfilled every cliché in the book by going to Paris for our first—a romantic weekend filled with macarons, art galleries, historic buildings and earnest conversations about how good our relationship was. Year two was spent in Washington, DC, walking around the Mall in the sun and taking selfies in front of the Lincoln Memorial. Year three we were home, but still went out to a fancy restaurant to celebrate, which was also true for years four and five. I can't remember doing anything past that point, as the diaper years descended upon us in a pile of tiredness and mess. It's not like we consciously decided not to. It just ceased to be a 'thing'.

When I think about anniversaries, part of me wants to slap my smug former self with her romantic Parisian jaunt. There's a photo of me draped from a lamp post, Eiffel Tower in the background. That girl didn't know that, one day, the height of romance was your partner saying, 'Leave the poonami to me, I'll clean it up.' She thought that the exact version of what she had would last forever, even though it couldn't. The dopamine hit never does.

I'd never ridden a horse before. Before the year of new things, the only ponies in my life were of the 'My Little' variety. I'm scared of horses: their height; their speed; their mouth of massive teeth; their neighing. It was the perfect anniversary gift—a new thing, something that pushed me out of my comfort zone, a fun thing to do together. Maybe it would even be romantic, à la our Parisian jaunt. Maybe I'd get a dopamine fix as I sat astride my noble steed.

The world was our oyster. Alan and I left our children with a babysitter, and off we went to celebrate eleven years of being married. Well, eleven years since we got married, as we had been separated during that time. But why complicate things by being pedantic? We had horses to ride after all.

Plot twist: it wasn't romantic. My horse bit another horse on the bum while I was sitting on it, and the subsequent jerking and neighing still haunts my dreams. I wondered whether the death card from the tarot reading was really an omen that I was going to meet a grisly end being stomped to death by an angry horse. Alan and I were placed at opposite ends of the trek line, so while I could see his helmeted head bobbing up and down in the distance, we didn't get to do anything romantic while riding. Although, in retrospect, I wasn't sure what romantic things I even had in mind. Reciting poetry in the sunset? Our horses galloping in unison to triumphant music? Afterward, our nether regions were sore for all of the wrong reasons. But it was still a neat thing to do together; once I had safely dismounted without dying, I decided it had been fun. Sometimes the memory is more fun than the moment, and this was one of those times. When we got home, we showed Jack and Dahla the photos and they were delighted by them, as well as the story of my horse biting another. They wanted a blow-by-blow account, and Alan and I delighted in sharing our experience with them. I snuck a glance at Alan as he told Jack about the horse he'd ridden, both of them basking in the glow of a good story.

*Here we are*, I thought. *Eleven years. And how lucky I am.*

And that's a different sort of romance. The dopamine is gone and things aren't always perfect, but it's still a pretty good happily ever after. Why? Because it's real.

I'd learned about what I needed to do to improve my relationship, including giving less of myself to other people when they weren't worth it. And, most of all, I'd realised how much I didn't want to see the death card again in a tarot draw about my future.

Will we last forever? Maybe, maybe not. This story is far from over and the script is still being drafted. But at least I know I'm committed to giving it my best shot, and sometimes that's all you can do.

And I've decided that's okay.

# 5
# PART-TIME MUM

✳ **New thing 25**: Going to a planetarium

✳ **New thing 26**: Making balloon animals

✳ **New thing 27**: Going trick-or-treating

✳ **New thing 28**: Going on the luge

✳ **New thing 29**: Having a child-free holiday

✳ **New thing 30**: Being a parent-helper

✳ **New thing 31**: Keeping a gratitude journal

✳ **New thing 32**: Going paddleboarding

**WHEN YOU'RE A PARENT, PEOPLE CHUCK** hurt-grenades in your direction on a regular basis. You can't do anything right. There is no winning. Some days, it feels like whatever parenting decisions you make, there is someone waiting with a pitchfork and torch to bang down your door and recite the reasons why you ought never to have had children.

When those days are particularly bad, my children and I eat Wacky Dinner instead of regular dinner. Wacky Dinner is wacky because it is actually breakfast food. My children think it's like Christmas. Breakfast for dinner! Wow! So much fun! I think it's like Christmas too. Actually, not really. I always end up doing a lot of cooking and dishes on Christmas, and the beauty of Wacky Dinner is the lack of both. Jack and Dahla love it, so it's a shame that I continue to feel guilty about being too tired to cook properly. Maybe that's the truly wacky part: that something can bring my children so much joy, yet still leaves me feeling like a failure. When you're a parent you are constantly being judged, and sometimes your harshest critic is yourself.

Add working motherhood to the mix and you open yourself up to a whole other level of criticism. Being a stay-at-home mother is tough. When I think back to my time at home with the children, it's a blur of laundry, bodily fluids, songs by The Wiggles and pushing a giant double buggy around the 'burbs while wearing activewear from Kmart. I have nothing but respect for women who perform this role for years on end.

Being a working mother is also tough. It's a constant battle that you can never win, not without sacrificing something in the process—your career, the ability to be a parent-helper for the school trip to the zoo, your health, your sanity. The internet is full of people spewing bile about how you should never have had children if you wanted other people to raise them, and that you are ruining your children's lives. To some people, if you willingly work when you could theoretically stretch your partner's salary to allow you to stay home full time, you might as well affix devil horns to your head. I hate to think what those same people would say if they knew that Wacky Dinner only ever happened after a long day of work.

Every now and then, someone will say something about my parenting that hits me between the eyes like a rusty spade.

'No kids need a part-time mum,' a man said once. 'You should be at home with them.'

Here comes the spade. Ouch. Part-time mum, as if my love for my children is so compartmentalised that I only wear it when not at work, like my old grey polar fleece, something that sits at home and only gets put on when I'm not doing anything else. Part-time mum, as if I only parent on the weekends.

Then there was the mum at Jack's school who made little comments about how I am rarely at the school gate, and 'joked' about me being a 'high flyer'. I say 'joked' because someone needs to tell this woman that actual jokes aren't made with such hard, unsmiling eyes. When this happens, I shrug and give a small smile, but on the inside I feel defeated and sad. I'm a part-time mum, unlike that other mum, who—in spite of being explicitly told not to by the school—makes a point of sending photographs to working mums of our children at school events. So we don't miss out, she says, being at work and all. I hear the criticism whether or not it's intended.

In my mind, there are two versions of me.

The first is the mother I want to be. She's the perfect mix of fun and stern. She cooks nutritious meals from scratch, so Wacky Dinner is actually something fancy and free-range that is arranged on the plate to resemble one of the Seven Wonders of the Modern World . . . which the children then name before eating, because they know all about such erudite things, rather than factoids such as the name of every Nexo Knight and a dozen words for 'bum'. This mother who I want to be engages her children in creative crafts without worrying about the mess, has kids who are rarely badly behaved, and is consistent with her punishment when they are. Her patience is like an infinite well. There is nothing she loves more than talking for hours and hours about the different types of dinosaurs, and she is able to suppress a giggle when her child asks if the man's seed that makes a baby goes in the mum's mouth. The question 'Why?' is like music to her ears, even after it's been repeated six hundred thousand times during a long car journey. She would never ever throw the Milky the Cow toy into the rubbish bin due to having to follow through on an ill-judged threat. (And then, after her daughter's subsequent meltdown, have to pick manky, rotten old orange peel off Milky so the bovine can be reunited with the aforementioned daughter without giving her the bubonic plague.) She's a perfect mother, this lady. She really is.

Then there's the other version: the version that I actually am. The one who loves her kids more than anything, but is still overwhelmed with nagging self-doubt about not doing the right thing by them at all times. The one who hears all of the criticisms, and worries that she's making the wrong decisions about pretty much everything. The one who reads that targeting a woman's parenting is, along with her looks, the thing that is most likely to trigger a shame response, and nods with recognition—but continues to feel the shame anyway.[1] It's too entrenched. She's the woman who hears the phrase 'part-time mum' and worries that it's true.

At the beginning of the year I wanted to do as many new things with my kids as I could. I had visions of the laughter we would share as we explored the world together. It would be all about #makingmemories and #feelingblessed. It would be #mumlife, but #mumlife in the stealth-boast way rather than the self-deprecating slummy mummy way. Oh, the photographs I would take of their beaming faces looking adoringly up at me as I continued my challenges! The fun! The things I would teach them that they would remember forever and pass to their own children!

After feeling like a part-time mum for so long, I was looking forward to making it up to them. Did I even have anything to feel bad about? Probably not. I saw plenty of my children and gave them my best self as much as I was able. But the guilt still nibbled away at the edges, so doing extra-special fun things with them felt long overdue.

Jack and Dahla were ripe for new experiences. All kids are. They're sponges, keen to soak up the world around them. **New thing 25**, going to a planetarium, was a raging success. Six-year-old Jack was fascinated by the fake shuttle launch. He asked all of the questions every parent secretly hopes their children will ask: why do some planets have rings and some don't? How hot is Mars? What makes the shuttle go up? He then asked some of the questions you'd never admit to other parents: what happens if you fart in space? Where does your poo go? Four-year-old Dahla got bored. But during the planet show, she snuggled up to me in one of those warm-fuzzy parenting moments you know you'll miss when they are lanky teenagers who ask you to park around the corner because the family car—and you—are *sooooo* embarrassing. I felt like a good parent that day. I decided that my year of new things would include more such moments. Jack and Dahla are the most important people in the entire world to me. I love them so completely and utterly that there is no way to put the feeling into words without resorting to cheesy clichés. Of course I would try to do as much with them as I could.

I was so proud of my idea for **new thing 26**, making balloon animals. Jack and Dahla love balloon animals. A day-care dad had learned how to do them, and had recently wowed the kids at a party. It looked so easy, too: just blow up the balloon, twist it a little, then—bam—an animal. I bought a 'balloon-modelling kit' and hatched grand plans that involved that activity being the centrepiece of our Saturday.

Mistake number one: not managing my children's expectations. If I had, they would not have been quite so disappointed when the giraffe looked like an inflated condom with eyes. Mistake number two: not squirrelling away the shiny leaflet displaying what balloon animals could be made by those more competent than me. That meant that my incompetence was painfully clear, as if the condom giraffe had not already underlined that fact. Mistake number three: not realising that the whole exercise wouldn't hold their attention for long.

'Can we watch TV now?' Jack said after fifteen minutes.

'No! We're doing new things together. We're making memories.'

'Can I make memories by watching TV?' he said.

Some of my new things with the children were more successful, but not for the reasons I'd expected. I took them trick-or-treating for **new thing 27**. I'd never gone before, and in the spirit of new things, decided to go. The kids loved it, although I don't know how much of that was about quality memory-making time with me and how much was about the stash of candy they got. And doing it was good for me, too. Another school mum I didn't know had arranged it, offering her house as a place to eat beforehand, and pre-planning which houses we should go to. It turns out this other mum works in my sector; another woman who is rarely at the school gates. She's fun and lovely and—I can see from the outside looking in—not a 'part-time mum' at all. She's just a mum who happens to work. Meeting another woman who was like me, especially someone who I'd get to know better over the course of the year, was worth the sugar rush my children were on for hours after we got home.

In the hope of making memories with the kids by doing fun and exciting things, **new thing 28** was a ride on the luge, a sort of go-kart toboggan thing that goes down the side of a hill. I went down the luge with Dahla perched between my knees. She was wearing her favourite dress, which was covered in llamas. Alan and Jack sped ahead, and Dahla started to cry.

'Catch them!' she cried. 'Daddyyyyy!'

When she wasn't crying, she was quiet, whimpering, 'I'm scared.'

'We're almost at the bottom,' I said, driving as slowly as I could without being a hazard. Defensive driving—fail. My luge spluttered to a total standstill, which set Dahla off again.

'Daddyyyyy!'

When we finally reached the bottom, she couldn't get out of the kart quickly enough.

'I did not like that,' she said, smoothing down her llama dress.

But then, a llama! There was an actual, real llama at the luge park. Dahla was delighted. She showed the llama her llama dress, proud as punch. She was happy again. I had seen a llama plenty of times, but Dahla hadn't, and certainly not while wearing a llama dress. That was the point at which I realised that if I was going to keep #makingmemories with my children, it didn't necessarily have to be about 'new' things. The kids may be sponges for new experiences, but they're only little, and pretty much everything is new for them.

On aeroplanes, they say you need to put on your own oxygen mask before you can help others, and I think this is true for parenting: if we can't breathe, we're useless. Those naff sayings people share online in swirly fonts with sunset backgrounds are right: self-care *is* important. It wasn't that the new things were good for my children. Not directly. But the new things made me happier, which made my parenting better, because my internal well of patience deepened.

For **new thing 29**, I put on my oxygen mask by going on my first child-free holiday since having kids, to Melbourne. It came at a good time. I was still reeling from the year that had come before; my mental health wasn't good. At the time, I had thought I was fine. I wasn't—I was lying to myself. But that trip was healing. It was such a treat to stay in a crisp hotel room where everything was white and soulless and clean instead of being covered in Lego or food or Lego covered in food. I could nap when I wanted, and didn't have to do chores. I wandered for hours up and down the river alone, thinking-but-not-really-thinking, feeling the essence of who I was seeping back. I came back home rested and much more at peace. Without a doubt, I came back a better parent. The toy kangaroo and koala helped, too. Especially the kangaroo. Dahla named hers Murray like the Wiggle, and slept with him in her bed every night for a week.

Towards the end of my year of new things, I decided to take the oracle's advice and slow down. Did that advice come from the spiritual world that she has a direct-line to, or was she merely an empath reacting to how worn out I looked? It doesn't matter. She was right either way. I wouldn't have gotten a facial tattoo or jumped off a cliff or dyed my hair blue if the oracle had told me to. And, like *The Tarot Bible* says, tarot is about being more self-aware, not telling the future.[2] I probably only remembered that advice because it worked for me. Nonetheless, I made a big decision, with Alan's full support. I was going to have some time without work again. No more being what some would call a part-time mum for me—I was going to be a full-time stay-at-home mother again, at least for a little while.

I don't think you can win, not really. Being a working mum is hard, but being at home is hard, too. I loved spending more time with the children during my time not working. I was a bigger part of what was going on in their days, and spent more time talking about the things that mattered to them. I got to know their teachers a little better, and do things like attend cross country without worrying about having to rush back to work. I went to every single soft-play centre in the greater Wellington region. We sang and danced and read books. Then, a highlight: **new thing 30**, being a parent-helper. I did one trip for each child, and they were so pleased I was ashamed that I'd never done it before.

'Can I sit with you on the bus?' Dahla asked over and over on the morning of her trip. 'I am so exciting. I get to sit with you on the bus.'

'You *are* exciting,' I said. '*And* excited.' Then, for the umpteenth time: 'Of course I'll sit with you.'

'That's my mum,' Jack said to his best friend during his trip.

His best friend rolled her eyes. 'I know.'

'Just in case you forgot,' Jack said. 'My mum's here.'

My kids didn't want luge rides or to make balloon animals that looked like condoms with eyes—they just wanted me. They wanted me to be with them in body and in mind; paying attention, not glued to my phone. They wanted to tell me about whatever was on their minds, regardless of how repetitive those conversations might be.

And yet . . .

Being at home was hard. It had been over three years since my last stint, so there were things I'd forgotten in all my self-flagellation about being a part-time mum. For example, how it felt to become overinvested in the housework and cooking. When I was working, I was too busy to care too much. Not so when I was home. I got twitchy about a weird stain on the side of the bath that I couldn't remove. I'd forgotten that the battle to get to the bottom of the laundry should be a level in Dante's 'Inferno', given how soul-destroying it is. I'd also forgotten how making yourself look nice starts to feel like a bit of a waste of time, so personal grooming falls by the wayside, which only makes you feel worse. The first couple of weeks at home I embraced the woollen-slouchy-trousers-and-no-make-up look.

It felt good to not care about heels and stockings and tightly-fitted clothes. But after a little while I started to feel slobby. I missed having a reason to dress nicely and put on make-up.

I'd also forgotten the part of being a stay-at-home parent where Alan gets home after a busy day at work and I have to try really hard not to follow him around the house and talk, just to hear the sound of my own voice. I'd forgotten that while you spend more time with your children, it's not always quality time. My children fight with each other a lot. But after about a month of me being home they found a common enemy: me. The novelty of having me around had worn off. You're the worst mum in the universe, they told me after I'd overreacted to a whistle being blown in my ear. You're the worst mum in the world, they chanted in unison. I'd poured everything into the kids, but hadn't put on my own oxygen mask. The net result: no one was having a very good time. Especially the whistle. It had been ceremoniously placed in the garbage amidst the howling and general commotion. It was never retrieved—I'd learned my lesson after Milky the Cow.

I'd forgotten that when I'd worked I was lucky to work flexibly, so I still saw my children a decent amount. For **new thing 31** I jumped on the mindfulness bandwagon and kept a gratitude journal, which I started during my last two weeks of work and continued into my time at home. That notebook is filled with lovely little moments I shared with my children: outings, conversations, cuddles, laughter. All moments that had occurred while I was still working. I'd forgotten that it really is about quality, not quantity. It's about me not being distracted.

In a weird way, when I was working, it was easier to put my phone down and engage with the kids when I was with them. A little guilt goes a long way. Moreover, having slivers of time before and after work to run errands and do boring life-admin meant not having to do those things while trying to parent.

On the days when my oxygen mask hadn't been put on, I *was* a part-time mum while I was staying at home, just in a different way. I may not have been at work, but if I was sitting on the computer trying to do the internet banking while my child was trying to engage me in conversation, I was still only half-present. I was still part-time.

On balance, I loved being at home for that period of a couple of months. It was the gift of time when I needed it. The oracle was right: it did me the world of good, both physically and mentally. As time passes, the memories of the grind ebb away, but the memories of spending more time with my children remain. I think about the happy afternoon the three of us spent at one of the many soft-play centres we visited, not the tantrums when I refused to buy a giant slab of chocolate cake. I think about the school excursions, and how pleased I am to have done that while my kids were at an age when they still wanted to hold my hand, even though their friends could see.

But I was pleased to go back to work nonetheless. I missed wearing my nice clothes, and I was ready to define myself by something else again. Besides, I never was going to figure out how to remove that stain on the bathtub, or ever finish all the laundry. If I had stayed home any longer, it would have sent me up the wall. But I decided to use more of my annual leave for things like school excursions, because you don't get that time back. And I know that now.

For **new thing 32**, I went paddleboarding on a hired board. It was a beautiful, crisp day, and Dahla and Jack sat with Alan on the beach and watched me as I tried to stand on the board. I wasn't very good at it. In fact, the only time I managed to stand for a decent length of time was the moment Alan took a photo. Good timing for the win! (And that was my profile photo for ages . . .) Months passed—at least five or six. One day I was driving along the coast with the kids in the back seat.

'Mummy,' Dahla said. 'Remember that time that you stood on that thing in the sea?'

It took me a while to figure out what she was talking about; it had been quite some time, after all.

'Oh, the paddleboard?'

'Yes,' Dahla said. 'The paddleboard.'

'It was funny when Mummy fell off,' Jack said.

'Mummy,' Dahla said. 'Next time you stand on that thing, I want to come too.'

I smiled. Maybe, for all my learning about parenting and realising the importance of doing small, everyday things rather than big, exciting things, my new things had sown some seeds after all.

'Of course you can,' I said. 'Of course.'

# 6

# A FEW
# QUIET DRINKS
# AND A BIT
# OF BANTER

✳ **New thing 33**: Giving up alcohol for six months

✳ **New thing 34**: Eating a vodka-infused doughnut

✳ **New thing 35**: Learning to do pilates

**EVER NOTICED HOW, WHEN YOU'RE DOWN,** it's so easy to forget what makes you happy?

Some things always make me feel better: being in nature; singing in the car; dancing when no one over the age of six can see; reading to the children, them snuggled up on either side of me on the couch; seeing a good friend; a decent workout. But when I was feeling down, did I do these things? No. It's what I think of as the Downward Spiral of Suck, which I talked about in the chapter on looks on page 62—that when you're unhappy, the things that make you feel better are often the hardest things to do. The things that ultimately make you feel worse are easier. And it sucks.

We've all been there. Doing or eating the right thing feels too hard or too complicated. Lots of people turn to quick fixes and short-term pleasure hits. Like food. Pies followed by cake, followed by shame: shame at having no willpower; shame at feeling too full; shame at failing yet another eating regime when your jeans are already too tight. Exercise becomes pretty much impossible. As the Downward Spiral of Suck sucks you in deeper and deeper, it can become hard to even leave the house. Sometimes even brushing your hair and teeth takes the sort of effort one would need to summon to conquer Everest. Basic things like looking for things to laugh about fall by the wayside, which is why Google searches for jokes are at their lowest on Mondays.[1] When we're glum, it's all too easy to not do the things that will cheer us up again. Instead, we make poor choices, for, as sung by the wise trolls in *Frozen*, people make bad choices when they're sad or mad or stressed.

Before my year of new things I constantly made choices that impacted negatively on my mental health: not exercising; not going to bed early enough; not eating well. As the year of new things progressed, I got better at doing those things, but something still wasn't quite right. Then it hit me, like a beer bottle between the eyes: drinking alcohol was one of those poor choices as well.

This came as a genuine surprise to me. I barely drank. I'd go out for a few quiet drinks and a bit of banter, but that was it. Apart from a period at university involving shopping trolleys, a duck pond and leftover keg beer that had sat in the sun for two weeks, I've never been a particularly heavy drinker. I have one or two, but rarely more. Alan and I didn't drink together. He likes beer, but a dozen will last a couple of weeks. I have never drunk alone, either, and know many people who drink much more than me. No, I wasn't a drinker at all. No way. Of course it wasn't a problem . . .

At least, this used to be true. I'd rush home from work on a Friday night, keen to spend an evening watching television with Alan. Fridays were about letting Jack and Dahla stay up a little later than usual and eating takeaways for dinner. There was a chant I used to do with the children on a Friday: 'No work, no school, no crèche, just fun!' Jack and Dahla would grin and bang their fists on the table. Just fun! Then life shifted on its axis. Fridays became a night when I started to go out straight from work instead, after falling into a social group that drank quite heavily. At first it was every now and again, but at some point it turned into most weekends. I looked forward to it. After years of being home with kids, I felt like I was in the world again. It was fun. For the first time since my mid-twenties, I'd deliberately wear an outfit to work on a Friday that I wouldn't feel dowdy or uncomfortable in if I ended up in a club. I went out and laughed and bantered and danced. It made me feel alive. I loved it. Then after a while, whenever I'd go out, I'd end up feeling bad for days afterward. At some point, the whole experience had changed—I had just been too slow to realise it.

During the first half of my year of new things, alcohol was the silent partner in many of the things I did. I had more than a few drinks during my child-free trip, **new thing 29**. One of the girls I was with had been alcohol-free for eight months after realising she had a drinking problem. She told me about her journey and I listened with interest, but as an outsider to the problem. I was months away from making the realisation about my own drinking. Wearing my bright red lipstick required Dutch courage. The group I set up was called 'wine and Netflix', not 'milk, cookies and Netflix'.

The list goes on. For someone who apparently only ever had a few quiet drinks over a bit of banter, alcohol was playing an increasingly significant role in my life. I could have continued to lie to myself about this. Alcohol consumption is a pretty easy thing to lie to yourself about. Almost one in five New Zealanders are classed as 'hazardous drinkers'.[2] Drinking is like changing your sheets or cleaning your bathroom: if someone asks you how often you do it, it's hard to remember exactly. So you respond with what you *think* is true, which is probably closely aligned with what you *want* to be true. Because of this, no one ever really knows if they are 'normal' or not. You think you must have changed your sheets the previous Sunday, even though you're not totally sure. Just like you had four standard drinks last week. Or was it six? Or maybe even eight? You can't quite remember.

Comparing yourself to other people doesn't work either. Even if you're in the realm of 'normal' and everyone else drinking the same amount as you is fine, it doesn't mean it's good for you. I know many people who drink so much more than me. I'm no Barney Gumble. Even at my worst, according to an online test, I was only at 'medium risk' of having a problem with alcohol, scoring 11 out of a possible 40 points.[3] It doesn't matter what that test says, though. One of the questions asks: how often in the last year have you had a feeling of guilt or remorse after drinking? Seeing this question in black and white still makes me feel ashamed. There were so many little moments I felt remorseful about. The money I'd spent, and all of the 'no work, no school, no crèche, just fun' chants I'd missed while doing something that didn't enrich my life in any way, shape or form. Remorse about the times I'd spent a Saturday sleeping to catch up after a night out, when it was lovely and sunny and I ought to have been outside doing things that energised me. Remorse for lowering my defences, meaning I was more likely to feel glum in the days following a night out. Worst of all was the lack of sleep, not just from the late night, but because I never slept deeply when I'd been drinking. I have Jack and Dahla; they wake up early. It wasn't like when I was young and could sleep until noon, and eating cold pasta kept the dry horrors at bay. When you're a parent and lose a night of sleep, it can take weeks to catch up. *Weeks*. It didn't matter what the tests told me. Going out was bad for my mental health. In his book on addiction, Russell Brand writes that one way to know whether you have a problem is to take a moment and ask yourself whether this thing is serving you, and whether you are happy.[4] 'A few quiet drinks and a bit of banter' was not serving me. I was not happy. It was time to change.

How then to pull myself out of that rut? In her book *This Naked Mind*, Annie Grace draws the distinction between the conscious and unconscious minds, and argues that we've been programmed to think we enjoy drinking on an unconscious level, which makes it all the more difficult to cut back. This is also why, even though we know, rationally, that it's bad for us, we can't stop.[5]

I decided to stop drinking after one specific night out. As nights out go, it was fairly run of the mill—nothing particularly momentous had happened. Yet I still woke the next day with a vague sense of dissatisfaction. I had the nagging feeling that the jokes I'd told a table of people I barely knew weren't funny, and I felt like a dick. I'd spilt my drink on someone, and I'd bickered with a friend in Burger King at 2 a.m. Something had been said that had unsettled me, but I couldn't quite remember the specifics of the conversation. My favourite silk dress reeked of cigarette smoke, and I was tired and in a bad mood. A switch flicked in my mind. The next day I decided I wasn't going to drink anymore; my *conscious* mind had made a decision. My rational self was on board with the plan. And it was fairly easy, until another Friday about six weeks later when it was hot and the cider was cool and the air prickled with that Friday buzz that infects the city sometimes. I didn't even consciously think about it; my rational self had gone on holiday. Next thing I was having a cider, then a few margaritas, then the hours passed and I was singing karaoke in a seedy bar well past midnight.

The next day my bestie George, who I hadn't seen in two years, was visiting from London. The visit had been in my calendar for months. As I drove to meet him, I felt seedy and grumpy and tired. When you've had too much to drink, even a scalding hot shower doesn't make you feel clean. I don't know what the scientists say, but it certainly feels like the toxins are still seeping from your pores the next day. George and I went for brunch, but I wasn't good company. I was too tired. I told him I'd been out the previous evening. We reminisced about the drinking and dancing and other fun times we'd had at university, still bonding over shared alcohol experiences almost twenty years after the fact.

We didn't reminisce about the underbelly of those nights out though: the #metoo moments; the time George rode with me in an ambulance to A&E after I took a fall at a club; the time he fell through a glass window. The time George found me asleep on the street after a night of cheap bourbon, totally oblivious to the two girls standing over me, poking me with sticks. 'I think it's alive,' George heard one of them say before poking me some more. 'I don't think it's dead.' People never reminisce about these sorts of things. If they do, the stories are spun as a funny yarn. Talking about the bad side of drinking isn't part of the bonding-over-alcohol code we've all unwittingly subscribed to.

'That was so long ago,' George said. 'I can't believe you're still having nights out. How do you do it?'

Was it admiration or judgement? I couldn't tell.

'I don't know,' I said.

'Did you fall asleep on the ground and have some random girls poke you with sticks?' he asked.

Okay. Maybe he was comfortable talking about that memory after all.

After brunch, George came back to my house, as he would be staying with me for a few days. I slipped away to have a sleep; I couldn't stay up any longer. As I drifted off I could hear George chasing the children around and playing monsters, Jack and Dahla screaming in delight. I wanted to join them, but I wanted to puke even more. Sobriety: fail. It was time to renew my teetotal vows, at least for long enough to change my habits. **New thing 33** would be giving up booze for six months. Completely.

Society is obsessed with booze. It's so normalised that most people hardly even notice it. I didn't, not until I tried to give it up. When I was pregnant it was easy: my desire to grow a healthy baby kept my rational mind front and centre. This time was different. I liked a tipple, and had no extra motivation of the growing-a-baby variety. The crappy, regretful feeling of doom or being tired or having my mental health go south were all things that were easy to forget when it was 6 p.m. on a Friday, I was in a pub and everyone else was having a beer. Especially if I was feeling bad about myself, so the Downward Spiral of Suck had been activated with full dastardly force.

Booze is everywhere. It's a fixture at pretty much every social thing I go to. Even in mum-land it's all wine this and gin that. Facebook memes tell me: 'Don't forget to pick up a bottle of wine for your mother on Mother's Day. After all, you're the reason that she drinks.' 'The most expensive part of having kids is all the wine you have to drink.' 'Gin and tonic: Mummy's Little Helper.' And most places don't cater very well for non-drinkers. There are the usual fizzy drinks but, in many places, there's nothing else. For every trendy bar with a delicious virgin mocktail, there's somewhere else selling flat Diet Coke. Or, in the case of one event I went to, a can of Coke that was two years past its expiry date.

I wasn't drinking, but there was a loophole to be exploited in the word *drinking*. Did it count if the alcohol was *eaten* instead of drunk? No one ever failed a breath test after eating too much tiramisu. Nor does brandy-laced Christmas cake lead to singing the Spice Girls at 3 a.m. in a karaoke bar. Black Forest gateau has never given me a hangover. Surely it didn't count to eat alcohol? Then Mum had an idea. She'd heard about this new cafe in town that sold something she'd love to try—vodka-infused doughnuts! *What a good idea*, I thought. It was much more socially responsible than actual drinking, not to mention it was in the spirit of new things. And as it was suggested by Mum, of course it was fine. She isn't a brazen booze-hag by any stretch of the imagination. Thus: **new thing 34**, eating a vodka-infused doughnut.

Mum and I went to the cafe one sleepy Sunday afternoon and ordered a pile of sugary doughnuts. They came with giant vodka-filled syringes that we squirted into the doughy mass of joyous rapture. They were divine. But, eating alcohol really isn't the same as drinking it, and I preferred the doughnuts filled with chocolate to the vodka ones. Not that it mattered what we were eating; it was just a lovely afternoon. Mum got diagnosed with stomach cancer not long afterward, and her stomach was removed. She can't eat much at all now, let alone that sort of food. I'm glad my new things motivated us to have such a nice afternoon together. Sometimes, you don't realise you're on borrowed time until it's too late. You don't realise that your window to eat vodka-infused doughnuts with your mum is limited, and that, if you don't seize the day, you may never have another chance.

The months passed. I remained teetotal. And sometimes it was really difficult. At first I didn't want to tell anyone I wasn't drinking. Partly because I hadn't completely decided what my end goal was, and partly because I didn't want to make a big thing out of it then get snapped in a bar with a cider in my hand. I'd failed in my first attempt, after all. Ordering a Coke when everyone else was having beer made me feel self-conscious, especially when people said 'What, you're not having a drink?' in the same tone of voice you'd expect them to use for 'What, you like to sniff dirty underpants?'[6] It makes some folk uncomfortable when you don't drink. They get defensive, especially heavy drinkers who want to be enabled. These people hear your sobriety as criticism. I used to be like that. One night out, not long before I gave up, a friend had said they wouldn't be drinking as they wanted a good sleep and had a lot they wanted to get done the following day.

I said: 'Good for you.'

I thought: *She's judging me! Is she judging me? I have lots to do tomorrow too, am I making bad decisions? No, I'm not. I'm just having fun . . . Oh no, is the night going to be really lame now she's not drinking? Will this fun night I've been looking forward to turn into a repeat of that downer evening when someone ended up playing Johnny Cash? Depressing Johnny Cash, not upbeat, country Johnny Cash? Oh no. I respect that she's not drinking. Of course I do. But I wish that she would have just one . . .*

Other people were simply surprised I wasn't drinking, which mortified me. I'd never intended to be that party girl what everyone expects to have a drink in her hand. I got sick of the comments, so I started driving to events on purpose. Driving is sacrosanct. It is—along with pregnancy—the only reason for abstaining that does not get questioned. Dangling your car keys is the one way to get the naysayers to leave you alone.

Some evenings, it was really hard not to drink. Wine and beer both smell really good sometimes. Not always. A certain wine or beer smell can bring back traumatic memories of bad hangovers, or that disgusting stench that lingers in dingy old pubs. Other times, though, wine and beer smell like Fridays. They smell like fun and laughter. They smell like the word

'Ahhhh' would smell if it wasn't just a word. When I first arrived somewhere and the booze started flowing, I would always, without fail, have a moment of really, really wanting a drink. This never stopped happening, the whole time I wasn't drinking, and it never got any easier. And there was always a good reason to partake. It was Friday. I was celebrating someone's birthday, or seeing friends, or whatever other reason we had for getting together. It had been a good week—what better way to mark it than by having a drink? It had been a bad week—what better way to mark it than by having a drink? Whatever non-alcoholic drink I had in my hand never quite hit the spot. Yet, I persisted. After a few hours, as the people around me loosened up, my desire for a drink also passed.

Most of the time, being sober didn't affect my fun. When everyone else was laughing, I laughed too, regardless of my blood-alcohol levels. The banter flowed just the same. I danced and sang and chatted, just with more control. Then, at some point, the people around me got drunk and annoying. It was the point at which people lost their sense of personal space and other boundaries. It was the point at which a woman I barely knew told me about her and her husband having mismatched libidos. It was the point at which you could smell what people had been drinking when they talked to you. And, more interestingly, it was also the point at which my friend that I used to have awkward late-night conversations with started being obnoxious and tried to pick a fight. I used to be so confused and upset the day after these conversations, as I'd never understood how they'd come about or what my part had been. Now I wondered if she'd been drunkenly picking fights the whole time. At this point of the evening, I would leave. When I got back in my car, I would always think: *I'm glad I didn't drink tonight.* Then, when I got into bed and thought about the evening I'd had, the same thought popped into my head: *I'm glad I didn't drink tonight.* This sense was amplified a million times over the next morning, and would last for the entire weekend. Instead of that icky feeling of not quite remembering a situation or the seedy feeling of having had too many wines, I'd be up with the kids, feeling as rested as one can ever feel with two children, and proud of myself for abstaining.

There were downsides to not drinking. At one party, I drank so much Coke Zero I was home by midnight but couldn't sleep until 3 a.m. The next day I felt seedy and dehydrated and tired, just like I would have if I'd been drinking booze. The next evening out I stuck to water, but needed to pee so often the people I was with must have thought I had some sort of infection. These were minor things, though. After two months of not drinking, for **new thing 35**, I signed up to learn how to do pilates, which one of my new online friends had suggested. My body was creaky and I needed to strengthen my core.

The class was once a week, at 9.30 a.m. on a Saturday. Old me wouldn't have given the idea a second thought. Of course I wouldn't do it. Even one glass of wine on a Friday would make me less keen on pilates the next day, as it would affect my sleep. But now I could do it. I'd reclaimed my Saturday mornings. After pilates I would drive home with some lunch from the bakery: something for Alan and me, some gingerbread men for Jack and Dahla. And again I would think: *I am glad I did not drink last night.*

Without trying, I also began to lose weight. I hadn't expected that at all, but I shouldn't have been surprised. The alcohol, the 2 a.m. burger, the tiredness and subsequent illness—they all triggered the Downward Spiral of Suck, aka my inability to make good choices when I'm feeling poorly. It's not rocket science of Nobel Prize-winning proportions to say that a Saturday morning pilates class was better for me than a greasy pie for breakfast. During that period my weight reached the lowest point it had been since having children, which was made even more awesome by the fact I was still eating plenty of treats. I was just eating them at three in the afternoon, when I savoured every bite, rather than at times when I didn't. By the time I decided to drink again, I could fit into a dress I hadn't worn since getting pregnant, which made me want to start a ticker-tape parade in honour of my disappearing back flab. I wore the dress out proudly one night, sipping on my mocktails and feeling like the bee's knees. I felt like I was winning.

In the end, my new thing of giving up alcohol lasted six months. I went for a walk with a good friend, and just felt like a drink. We went to a pub afterward, and I thought: *It's time.* I had a cider, and it was good. Then I had a second. But, unlike before, I didn't fancy a third. Unlike before, two was enough.

Giving up drinking wasn't a forever thing; I'd never intended it to be. It was a lesson in moderation. When there is a certain buzz in the air and the smell of wine or beer hits my nostrils, I'll have a drink, and I'll enjoy it. But, now I know how good it feels to wake up the next day without regret, I always stop before getting to a certain point: I rarely go past two, and have not drunk more than four since. When I'm at work on a Friday and someone suggests a drink, sometimes I go, and I usually have a good time. I have a few quiet drinks and a bit of banter, but without regrets. And sometimes I still stick to the Coke and water. But most of the time, all I want to do after work is go home. And on those days I sit at the table with Jack and Dahla, and we bang our fists on the table. No work, no school, no crèche, just fun! And I have never once regretted being with them instead of being out. My friends may offer a few drinks and a bit of banter, but they can't chant half as well as my children, and that's more important.

# 7

# BEING A
# CLASSY
# LADY

❋ **New thing 36**: Learning to play a song on the piano

❋ **New thing 37**: Doing a watercolour painting class

❋ **New thing 38**: Learning a hip-hop dance routine

❋ **New thing 39**: Doing a cross-stitch

❋ **New thing 40**: Going to a cooking masterclass

❋ **New thing 41**: Riding a mechanical bull

**A MAN ONCE TOLD ME THAT** I wasn't as classy as the girl he was infatuated with, because I had enjoyed going to a specific underground dance club.

'She'd never go there,' he said. 'She's too classy for that.'

My first thought was an overwhelming feeling of being jabbed in the stomach with a poker dipped in pain sauce. Ouch. My second thought was confusion. It was a great club. Once, they even played 'The Time Warp'. 'The Time Warp'! The dance floor was heaving with women of my age and life stage. What's not to like? The self-doubt then began to seep in; that niggling thought that I was somehow deficient. This wasn't the first time that the term 'classy' had, when used by a certain kind of man in reference to me *not* being classy, made me feel like I had failed in my womanly duties. Isn't 'classy' a synonym for 'feminine', after all? While this kind of thing may be disguised as banter, it's not funny. Like comments about mothering or looks, it hits at the very heart of your gender identity.[1]

What, then, does classy even mean?

I've always understood that 'classy' is different from 'dignified'. Dignified is more about your integrity and how you hold yourself. Dignity personified is Michelle Obama when she said, 'When they go low, we go high.' Dignity applies to men and women, the young and the elderly. Dignity is considered a universal human right. It is something that can be given by allowing someone else their dignity. It is also something that you yourself can hold close, by how you react to what life throws at you.

The concept of 'classiness' is murkier. To be described as classy by a certain kind of man, it seems that the most important prerequisite is to be good-looking, at least conventionally so. A classy woman needs to dress well, ideally in a feminine manner. It's also important to be thin. In something I can only describe as fat-shaming by stealth, I don't think I've ever heard of a non-thin person being described as classy. It also helps if you are posh, aloof, cold, shy or reserved. But, even then, I still don't know what it really means. I know some women who are considered classy because of their poise and ability to exude a quiet air of something special. I also know some quite unpleasant women who have that toxic combination of good looks and aloof arrogance that also puts them into the classy category. Like I said, it's murky.

I do understand what *isn't* considered classy. If you want to be seen as classy you don't talk about bodily functions, use the 'c' word or snort while you laugh. You don't drink beer quickly and then burp. You must also never, under any circumstances, stray from the maiden-mother-crone narrative. I'd heard about the maiden-mother-crone thing when I was in my late teens, and thought it was a pile of bollocks. *We're all complex beings, we women, it's ridiculous that we'd be put in three categories like that,* I thought. But we are by some people. Before we have children, we're not classy unless we act like a maiden. And, once we do, we can't be described as classy if we stray from the narrative about what a mother ought to be. I love being a mother. I am blessed to have given birth to two such fabulous beings, and know how very lucky I am. That goes without saying. They have changed the trajectory of my life for the better. After I had Jack and Dahla, though, it took me a little while to realise the way people perceived me had also changed. I'd never really felt like a maiden—I knew I wasn't classy enough—but all of a sudden I'd transitioned to 'mother' and realised that whatever I'd been seen as before was gone. I felt invisible as a stay-at-home mother. You don't realise how visible you were until you are no longer seen; not physically, but as an individual. Maybe it was the fact my buggy was identical to the one most other women in my suburb pushed around. Maybe it was my unkempt hair and tired expression. It could have just as easily have been the cheap activewear that I wore. Whatever the cause, after I had children, for a long time I felt like all of my life achievements meant nothing. All that mattered were my parenting choices. I was no longer that woman with a master's degree and a career, I was the woman who had made the most disgusting baby puree in the entire history of baby puree. When I first went back to work after a significant period of time at home after Jack was born, Alan did a stint as a stay-at-home dad. One Saturday I was at the supermarket with baby Jack, and a checkout operator I'd bought groceries from countless times over the past months smiled at him.

'Where's your daddy?' she said. 'You're usually with your daddy.'

All those times buying food from her and chatting about the sort of mundane details you talk to checkout operators about, and she'd never once noticed me.

Even when Jack and Dahla were a little older and I re-emerged once again into the world of work, my transition to 'mother' was something I was reminded of in the unlikeliest of places. A male friend once told me I was 'gross' to talk about finding Justin Timberlake hot.

'Why?' I asked, genuinely surprised. Did this man not possess eyes? Could he not see?

'Because you're a mum,' he said.

During a conversation with a second male friend, I'd told him about a nineties dance party I'd gone to with a bunch of other mums I'd met online.

'You can't go out like that,' he said. 'You're a mother now.'

'What?' I said.

'You're a bunch of mums. It's gross.'

Gross? To be fair, dancing to Hanson's 'MMMBop' followed by some frenzied moves to S Club 7 probably *was* a little gross, but that had nothing to do with our reproductive history. At first I thought the man was joking, but he wasn't. We are maidens *or* mothers *or* crones. I assume he thought I should be spending my evenings trying to perfect that baby puree or something equally boring. It seems you shouldn't talk about sex either, especially once you've had children. It's not ladylike; not *classy*.

And where does the term 'classy' even come from? Did men start describing women as classy when they realised it was frowned upon to call them 'a lady' or 'ladylike'? Historically, what one required to be 'a lady' was much clearer. There were finishing schools you could attend, and strict rules about what you could not do. Sticking out your pinky while drinking tea was ladylike. Sticking up your middle finger when someone bothered you was not.

On a rational level I knew that I didn't like the idea of being classy or ladylike. My anti-classy rant as detailed above was well-practised. So much so that anyone who knows me well has probably skipped the last three pages as there wasn't anything there that they hadn't heard before. Yet—deep down—I also wanted to be called classy. Have you ever heard of cognitive dissonance? It's the psychological term used to describe wanting two things that are in contradiction with each other, or having inconsistent beliefs. Examples include smoking when you know it's bad for you, wanting the pool boy to return your crush while also hoping to strengthen your marriage, and— in my case—thinking the concept of classiness is a pile of bollocks, yet still wanting to be considered classy all the same. It's uncomfortable, cognitive dissonance. You always know, deep down, when thou doth protest too much. Rational, time-warping Lauren didn't want to be classy, but hidden, awkward, inner Lauren did. Two-thirds of the way through my year of new things, I had an idea. I could use my new things to try to harness my inner lady! I would try some traditional ladylike pursuits. Maybe being classier, more ladylike, could be part of my rewritten script. I liked the idea. It could be a whole new me. A classier version.

But where to start?

In *Pride and Prejudice*, the Bingleys and Mr Darcy have a conversation about what makes for an accomplished woman. Miss Bingley says: 'A woman must have a thorough knowledge of music, singing, drawing, dancing, and the modern languages, to deserve the word.' As I figured 'accomplished' was just another way of saying 'classy', this seemed as good a place as any to begin my quest for classiness.

First on the list: music. For **new thing 36** I taught myself to play a new piece of music on the piano. With both hands! Not 'Chopsticks', either. An actual piece of music, that involved reading music and practice. It took some effort; I hadn't learned to play a piece of music like this in over twenty years. It took about a month of regular banging away at the keyboard. It was hard, but satisfying. There's something very cool about marking your progress and turning random black squiggles on paper into something that sounds nice. I was also glad to have a keyboard that I could plug headphones into. I imagine the neighbours were equally pleased. Our houses aren't that far apart and hearing the same chords over and over wouldn't have given them much aural pleasure.

Next: singing. I looked into singing lessons for one of my new things and found someone who would teach me. But then I chickened out. Isn't vulnerability a strange thing? I had been able to do all of these other things during my year but was too nervous to do a singing lesson. There was something too intimate about the whole thing. I did sing a lot while in the car, though. In my imagination, that's just like warbling a dainty tune in a Georgian drawing room while tapping away on the pianoforte. And, of course, we can't forget my karaoke rendition of 'I Will Survive' during my last big boozy night out before I gave up alcohol for a while. It was still singing, and I like to think that counts. It's ladylike AF.

Drawing, the third on the list, was **new thing 37**. Or, more specifically, a watercolour class with a girl from work. I didn't know her well, but she knew I was looking for new things to do, and had invited me to join her. It was a nice way to spend an evening: painting and chatting to someone I'd only known in passing before. I also learned how to carry a wet painting home on the bus without getting any paint on my light brown coat. I don't know how I managed it, but wouldn't dare try again. I wouldn't want to tempt fate.

Dancing was the most energetic of all of my womanly accomplishments. What maiden of grace and beauty wouldn't want to learn a distinguished La Boulanger or waltz? Or . . . hip-hop? For **new thing 38** I learned a hip-hop routine. Maybe it wasn't the best dance style to learn while aiming to be classy. There was thrusting and shaking. I figured that it was still true to Miss Bingley's list, though. When she talked about what made for an accomplished woman, she didn't specifically mention that they couldn't do pelvic thrusts, did she? No, she did not. In fact, who's to say that she wouldn't have thought a bit of booty shaking was the perfect addition to a set of the quadrille at a country assembly hall?

Lastly: modern languages. I didn't do a new thing based on modern languages, but I hope it won't matter. After all, when I was eighteen I lived in Italy for a year. While there I went on a camp with teenagers from all over the world. We spent an entire evening teaching each other a dozen different ways to say 'shit'. I am sure that goes well above and beyond what Miss Bingley had in mind.

I also did other ladylike things. **New thing 39** was doing a cross-stitch. It was of a camel. Such a ladylike animal, the camel. The camel cross-stitch reminds me of how regal and classy I was when I rode a camel in Egypt. Well—maybe not ladylike per se. I'd had a total brain-fart that day and worn a skirt, so I spent most of the ride with one hand on the reins and the other holding my skirt down so I didn't accidentally flash the guide. Then, when the ride was finished, the guide made the camel get down on one knee only, leaving me half-dangling from the beast.

The guide turned to Alan. 'I'll let her to the ground when you give me more of a tip.'

My clear articulation to Alan of the necessity of prompt payment to the guide was not terribly ladylike either. But, cross-stitch of a camel! That's a whole other story. It took months, but I was so proud of the end result it is framed on my wall—unlike the watercolour, which I prefer to keep in the cupboard.

For **new thing 40**, I took a cooking masterclass. During my adult life I've often felt like my womanhood was somehow lessened by my competent yet average cooking. Especially baking. My sister and mum make and decorate cakes that are edible art. Not me. For years, whenever I needed to bake something, I would slink off to the supermarket and buy biscuits instead, presenting them on a plate and muttering about being out of flour at home. This sense of inadequacy and shame motivated me to do a cake-making and decorating course when Jack was a baby. It also caused me to go through phases of buying glossy cookbooks, deluded that I might actually make more than one recipe inside. Because cooking was so interlinked with my sense of womanhood, I was surprised to find that all of the instructors on the masterclass were men. I felt daft for having assigned gender to the skill in the first place. I also got to eat some delicious treats, and it was an interesting way to spend a Saturday. And did I mention the trick to peeling tomatoes I was taught? I left motivated to try it at home. It was a shame that by the time I got around to acquiring tomatoes for peeling, I'd completely forgotten how.

As the year ended, I wondered whether I was any more ladylike, any more classy. The answer was a resounding no. Of course I'm not; I'm still me. I may have done some of the things on Miss Bingley's list, but she also said that, to be accomplished, a woman must 'possess a certain something in her air and manner of walking, the tone of her voice, her address and expressions'. I don't even know where you'd begin in trying to achieve those things, especially as they are so subjective. I wonder what 'expressions' she even means. The rapt expression a woman might adopt while listening to a mansplainer? Or perhaps she meant the sort of terrified expression I wore while doing **new thing 41**, riding a mechanical bull? Now that was classy. Or at least it was once I'd borrowed someone's jeans after trying to ride the bull in a short dress in a bullish reenactment of my camel ride from years ago. I don't know if I possessed 'something in my air', but I was certainly not on the bull for long before literally being *in* the air. That's pretty much the same thing, right?

Trying to do those things put my cognitive dissonance to bed; I no longer had that little voice in my head that thought it wanted to be called classy. There were no internal contradictions to grapple with anymore, as I'd fallen clearly on one side of the ledger and firmly decided that talking about traditional womanly pursuits is stupid. Unless something specifically requires the use of one's reproductive organs, surely it's unisex by default? And if a new thing requires the use of one's aforementioned organs, it's not the sort of new thing I want this book to be about, even though *52 Shades of New Things* would be a catchy title. Besides, both men and women cook and play music and sew and paint. Poor Miss Bingley. She and her 'accomplished woman' spiel need to get with the programme. If that scene had happened now, I like to think Elizabeth Bennet would have rolled her eyes and told her future in-law to stop being so insecure and betraying the sisterhood in the process.

I also think that there is certain sort of man who will never call me 'classy'. No amount of cross-stitch will change that. But I don't mind. That's their problem, not mine. I enjoyed trying these new things for other reasons. Playing the piano and doing cross-stitch forced me to entertain myself without staring at a screen, and were surprisingly relaxing. Especially the piano playing. It reminded me how much I enjoy losing myself in a piece of music. Playing the piano also made Jack and Dahla more curious about it, so I ended up digging out my old 'learn to play' book from when I was a kid and going through the basics with them. Watching Jack plod away at his 'Every Good Boy Deserves Fruit', I smiled and thought that this is the sort of parent I want to be.

The watercolour class was relaxing as well. The painting looked nothing like it was supposed to, but that's partly because I enjoyed stroking the brush up and down and up and down so much—it was hypnotic. It was so mindful I never wanted to stop, even if it made my sea look like it had a sewage pipe spewing waste into it.

I can do these things and still enjoy dancing to 'The Time Warp' in an underground club. And, while I'm dancing, I'll be happily putting the ass in class—and not letting my womanhood, or perceived lack thereof, be a stick that I allow people to beat me with.

And if that doesn't make me classy, who cares. I don't want it.

# 8

# LONELINESS, THE STEALTH NINJA OF FEELINGS

❄ **New thing 42**: Wrapping a giant
lizard around my neck

❄ **New thing 43**: Going go-karting

❄ **New thing 44**: Doing an escape vault

❄ **New thing 45**: Going to a political meet-the-
candidates event and talking to every candidate

❄ **New thing 46**: Going parasailing

❄ **New thing 47**: Going to a music festival alone

❄ **New thing 48**: Volunteering at a retirement village

**THE WORST THING ABOUT LONELINESS IS** that it comes on slowly.

It's not like you go to bed one night feeling loved, and then a switch is flicked and suddenly your own company feels like a millstone around your neck. Loneliness is sneakier than that—it's the stealth ninja of feelings. It eats away at you in increments, nibbling around the edges before it takes chunks out of your middle. You feel sad or ranty or randomly angry at the hapless stranger talking too loudly on the bus, but don't know why you feel that way. Your own company becomes something to be avoided rather than enjoyed. Solitude and loneliness might look exactly the same from the outside, but there's no solitude when you're lonely. Your own company isn't peaceful and relaxing. It's just empty.[1]

When you're lonely, things that used to bring you pleasure mock you for not doing so any longer. Simple things like coming home after a busy day at work feel heavy. Loneliness is hard on your sense of mental well-being. It leads to depression, and causes your mind as much stress as being punched by a stranger.[2] Loneliness is also hard on your body. It's as bad for you as being obese[3] or smoking fifteen cigarettes a day.[4] When we feel rejected, our immune system is more likely to be weakened, which, if sustained over a long period of time, can lead to severe illness.[5] Nineteenth-century philosopher Arthur Schopenhauer said: 'Life oscillates like a pendulum, back and forth between pain and boredom.'[6] This is a real downer of a quote, but, when you're lonely, it rings true.

If you're anything like me, food becomes your friend. It's a friend that fills up time: go to the supermarket, plan meals, go home, prepare food, eat. When food is your only friend, however, you can develop a pretty unhealthy relationship with it. And an unhealthy relationship with food can lead to some dire health implications.

Being lonely is hard to admit. It's embarrassing. If you say you're lonely, it feels like you're inviting everyone you know to do the 'L for loser' forehead sign with their finger and thumb whenever you enter a room. When you think about lonely people, a number of stereotypes spring to mind: misogynists dwelling in basements who spend their days trolling online forums; bearded hermits who live in hillside caves and have toenails that look like raptor claws; Tom Hanks in *Cast Away* with his best friend, Wilson the ball. We don't immediately think of people like me or you. If we don't conform to stereotypes, being lonely is something that is hard to recognise, even in ourselves. It's not something we talk about openly, so most people have no idea that 15–30 per cent of the population can be classed as chronically isolated.[7] And let's not forget that loneliness is the stealth ninja of feelings, so you often don't realise it's coming until you're choking in its solitary grip. You don't know it is coming until it's your constant and reliable companion.

It never occurred to me that what I was feeling was loneliness. How could it be? I had about 450 friends on Facebook, not a single piece of sporting equipment called Wilson among them. I get invited to plenty of things, and can make chit-chat like a pro. People who like me say I'm friendly and chatty. People who don't like me say I'm annoying and talk too much. Neither group would describe me as a raptor-clawed hermit covered in facial hair. Besides, how could I possibly be lonely when I was hardly ever alone? During the winter before my year of new things I couldn't even shower some days without little people ogling me through the glass. Nowhere in the house was sacred, not even the bathroom, because the lock had broken. On the days I had the kids, the only time I didn't have someone else with me was the ten-minute walk between the bus stop and home, which was often the highlight of my day. It never occurred to me that I could be lonely. I couldn't be lonely. I was standing in a crowd.

Shame specialist Professor Brené Brown writes about the stigma of loneliness. In her book *Braving the Wilderness: The Quest for True Belonging and the Courage to Stand Alone*, she says: 'Unchecked loneliness fuels continued loneliness by keeping us afraid to reach out.'[8] Indeed, my loneliness was unchecked. I was surrounded by people, but I didn't know how to tell them how much I needed them. I was too ashamed of feeling lonely to tell anyone how I felt, and wasn't seeing any of my friends often enough for them to figure it out for themselves. This wasn't their fault. They may have many talents but, to my knowledge, none are psychic. They can't read my mind. They couldn't have known how I was feeling if I didn't tell them. And I didn't. I didn't know how. Some conversations are too hard to start, and, once you start having them, they hurt too much. Sometimes it's easier not to say anything at all about the real stuff, so you chat instead about work, the weather and what the people you know in common are doing. Saying 'I think rain is coming' followed by some sage nodding is far more comfortable than telling someone that you are regularly overwhelmed by a wave of sadness that you don't know how to put into words.

I was also lonely because I didn't have as many friends as I used to. Not actual friends— people I could let down my guard with and be myself in front of. I had blinked, life happened, and then all of these former friends had somehow faded into the past, like a photograph that had been sitting in the sun too long. The weeks had become years, and there was all of a sudden less to say to each other whenever we did catch up. Friendships had undergone a seismic shift while I'd been living out my suburban-wife-and-mother script, and I didn't know what to do about it.

How, then, had these friendships changed?

Friendships, at least the healthy ones, aren't intense like they used to be. Unless you work with a friend, it's unusual to see someone more than a couple of times a month, if that. It isn't like school, when you see your friends every day. Nowadays, a catch-up every now and again is enough when you're in a relationship and busy with other things. It doesn't help that social media creates the illusion of knowing more about a person than you actually do. I was thinking about my best friend from school the other day, and decided that I really ought to contact her. I logged on to Facebook and read about her date night with her husband, her daughter's school project and then saw a photograph of her amazing new haircut. I 'liked' all of the posts and logged off. It was only later that it occurred to me that that didn't count as meaningful contact. We hadn't actually spoken—all I had done was press a button. Yet, after seeing those posts, the pressing need to get in touch was gone even though I was none the wiser about how she was *actually* getting on.

We can't just blame technology for friendships changing, though. There are a number of other reasons for this happening. Most people's bullshit-detectors get better with age, so friends who create too much drama or unnecessary angst are kept at arm's length. Even catch-ups with some of your favourite people in the world start with 'Has it really been that long since we last caught up?' and end with 'We must do this again soon', when you both know it's unlikely to happen again for months. As they get older, people—me included—become more discerning about how they want to spend their leisure time. In my early twenties, I would say yes to everything—and actually turn up! A weekend evening spent at home watching TV in my pyjamas only ever happened in the absence of other plans. Now it can be my perfect evening. If I need to recharge my batteries, I'll say no to invitations without hesitation. A lot of my friends are the same, especially those with young children. Like I said earlier, you've got to put on your own oxygen mask before you can help others. We are generally more aware of our needs, especially when rest is such a finite resource and you're more likely to fantasise about sleep than sex. Plus, we have so many reasons to stay at home now, as we live in the golden age of TV. When I was in my twenties, there was never anything good to watch on TV on a Saturday night. Now you can watch anything you desire, thanks to streaming services.

Making plans feels different now, too. People are constantly saying yes to things and then pulling out. It's as if they never actually intended to turn up in the first place, and just said yes to keep their options open. Yes is the new maybe, and maybe is the new no. Just ask anyone who's had 45 people accept a Facebook invite, then spent the evening with a handful of friends and a bunch of tumbleweeds. I get this, I do. Psychologists Yaacov Trope and Nira Liberman coined the phrase 'psychological distance' to explain how the greater the distance you are from the thing in question, the more abstract your information processing becomes.[9] This is why when someone asks you to their dinner party next month, you say yes right away. You've got no plans that month, and it sounds fun. You have psychological distance. It's only in the days beforehand that you remember it will take two trains to get there and think about how tired you are. You then decide that your top priority in life is to watch *Tiger King*, because you're only one of three people on the planet who didn't watch it during the Covid-19 lockdown and now you want to know what all the Carol Baskin memes were about. That's why the people I'd initially planned to go out with on the night of 27 Rejections of Doom thought it was a fabulous idea six weeks earlier, but were put off by the rain on the day. Or sickness. Or work. Or a myriad of other perfectly legitimate reasons that I totally understand, but still meant I spent that evening alone.

By the time I reached my mid-thirties it was as if most of the people who had been my urban family throughout my twenties had gone. Well, they weren't technically *gone*. With the exception of a few very sad cases they were still in the world. I saw their updates online, and bumped into them on the street where we had conversations about the need to 'do coffee' at some indeterminate point in the future. When we did see each other, I would so often be overwhelmed by just how much I still liked them and how I really ought to see them more. But we weren't spinning in the same orbits anymore. We were busy. We had other priorities. And I was lonely.

Easy, you might think. Old friendships have drifted away, so just make new friends, right? Wrong. Because the older you get, the harder it is to make friends. So, as old friendships drift away, they are often not replaced.

According to sociologists, there are three criteria that need to be met to make new friends: proximity; repeated unplanned interaction; and a setting that makes people comfortable enough to let their guard down.[10] These criteria are easier to meet when you're younger. It's so much harder to transition from acquaintance to friend when you're older, even with the people you see all of the time. Many people don't have the free time or the energy to cultivate new friendships. It takes time, time you don't want to give if you already have your set of old friends, a family, a demanding job and an addiction to Netflix. Since being a grown-up I've made friends in mums' groups and through work, but as the years pass, most friendships slowly drift away as soon as the proximity ceases. It's never on purpose, of course. I like these people; I wouldn't have become friends with them in the first place otherwise. After the thing we have in common dissipates—someone changes jobs or our children are no longer in the same class—we always *intend* to catch up, we really do. I never say 'let's do coffee' without meaning it. But, over time, the lunches and drinks become further and further apart, and then one day I'll think about the person and realise I haven't spoken to them for a year. Or, once you see each other less often, when you do catch up, the conversations become less about how you feel about things and more about superficial details of your lives. Or, even worse, your conversations become the mere swapping of notes about what so-and-so is doing now. This is the point it becomes clear you really don't have anything in common anymore. Especially if you are both Facebook friends with so-and-so and essentially reciting a third party's status updates to each other. 'Tis a dire state of affairs when one reaches that point—it's a friendship graveyard. No, I changed my mind. It's worse—it's the friendship zombie apocalypse. The friendship is akin to the undead, but instead of walking around screaming 'Brains!', you bump into each other on the street and earnestly promise you'll meet for a drink sometime but both know it's never going to happen.

I was so lonely that something had to change. My new things would be perfect for this, I thought: I would get to know people a little better by doing interesting things with them. For the first month of my year of new things, I contacted the friends I had been hiding from, and morphed into a womanly version of

Sam-I-Am in Dr Seuss's *Green Eggs and Ham*. I'm sure you know Sam-I-Am, the dude who constantly badgers the other guy to step out of his culinary comfort zone with his talk of boxes and foxes and so on. 'You do not like them, so you say. Try them! Try them! And you may.'[11] I was like a broken record: 'Do new things with me! It'll be fun! You know you want to!' I carried around my purple notebook in my handbag, keeping a list of ideas in the back. I diligently recorded the new things people suggested to me as well as the ones they said they would do. My purple pen captured in messy scrawl that the person I sat beside at work had always wanted to gut a fish ('Let's do it!' I said), three girls in my book club loved the idea of skydiving ('Of course we'll do that!' I said to them. 'Let's make a weekend of it!'), and my favourite aunt would teach me knitting ('Yes!' I said. 'I've never tried knitting! What a great idea!').

Some people had good ideas—things I never would have thought of myself. Many of my new things—dragon boating, paddleboarding, bouldering, hip-hop dancing, watercolour painting, the cooking masterclass—were ideas I got from other people based on things they liked to do themselves. When asking people about their interests and listening properly to their responses, you're given the gift of learning more about them. Folk I barely knew suggested new things that I didn't know they'd ever be interested in or liked to do. People don't talk about their hobbies that often, especially at work. Get someone chatting about something they're passionate about, though, and they transform into a whole different person.

We are all different things to different people. By the time we hit adulthood, most of us have learned enough situational versatility to adapt ourselves to whatever we might be doing. Unless you're really insecure or a closet narcissist, situational versatility isn't about being sneaky or fake. It's simply about not feeling comfortable enough to be vulnerable, or wanting to conform to social etiquette. My grey-polar-fleece-at-home self is different from my going-to-work-in-heels-and-a-dress self.

The other week, I was chatting to a woman at work. 'You always seem to wear dresses and skirts,' she said, out of the blue. 'Do you even *own* trousers?'

A few days later, I was at home with Dahla. She was wearing the sort of bright pink tutu that my pre-children self swore my future daughters would never wear. That was before I actually had kids, realised that my own biases were less important than letting my children be who they wanted to be, and chilled out. Dahla looked at my outfit and screwed up her nose.

'Why do you never wear dresses?' she said. 'Dresses are elegant. Your clothes are not elegant.'

Case in point. I'd never wear the grey polar fleece to work. No amount of tailoring would make that look halfway professional. My old bestie George calls it 'The Scab' and says that it will likely survive the apocalypse. Plus, it wouldn't fit with my work persona. It wouldn't assist with my situational versatility.

Situational versatility is more than what you wear. It's also about how you feed off the energy of the people around you. Before I had kids, I was a contractor in London. It was a great experience, and my love for London could fill a whole other book. Because I was a contractor, I changed jobs relatively regularly. Each job was quite different—different organisations, different people, different work content. After leaving one contract, the manager gave a particularly sweet speech.

'Lauren doesn't say much,' he said. 'She's very quiet. But when she does speak, we always listen.'

The farewell speech from my next manager was equally as sweet but had the opposite message.

'It will be so quiet without Lauren here,' he said. 'We'll miss her lively chatter.'

Not only was every job different, but apparently I was too, without even trying. Mind. Blown.

So why does this happen? At the risk of sounding like the Steve Urkel of psychology (as well as a complete, shameless nerd), I've been a longtime fan of Eric Berne's theory of transactional analysis to explain why we change depending on who we're interacting with.[12] He talks about the three ego states—parent, adult, child—and how we adopt one of those three states in reaction to the person we're interacting with. That's why someone giving a presentation to colleagues adopts a different state than the one they use to comfort a crying child or have a fight with their partner about how one ought to stack a dishwasher. That's why I was the 'quiet one' in one job, but the 'loud one' in the next.

Most of us are at least vaguely aware of our own inter-changeable personas. Sometimes painfully so. This is especially true in situations where your true self feels suppressed and self-editing makes you feel bad. Or when an old trigger turns you into a giant baby. For example, when you are celebrating

Christmas with your entire extended family and play a game you've been playing since you were kids, and you lose. Then, instead of being a cool, calm and collected adult, you sulk and sit in the corner and silently glare at everyone for being dirty cheaters, just like that time in 1992. Whatever the reason for the change, we usually feel the shift in persona ourselves. We know when we metaphorically (or, in my case, literally) change into a polar fleece nicknamed 'The Scab' as soon as we get home. We also know when we feel misunderstood, misrepresented or unfairly judged: this is not who we *really* are, can't the other person just *see* that? We often don't appreciate other people's situational versatility though.[13] We think that the people around us are exactly who they seem to be, and that we are good judges of character. It can be jarring to be proven wrong. Like when I was a kid and saw my teacher at the supermarket buying toilet paper. My egocentric young mind totally boggled. Not only did my teacher have a life outside of teaching me, but she also had a butt! Wow. Who knew? Indeed, when it comes to other people, we so often don't know what we don't know. We take things at face value without looking any further.

Talking to people about their hobbies and what they will and won't do is a window into a different version of themselves. A friend suggested that I try beekeeping with him as one of my new things. Bees! I hadn't had a clue he was a beekeeper, much less that his hive was overseen by one Queen Bey. The weather never worked out for us to do it, but it was neat to find out that he had it as a hobby in the first place. I still intend to try it with him sometime. I also found out that a woman who sat near me at work had a giant pet lizard. It was over 40 centimetres long and looked like a snake with legs. His name was Didgeridoo, Didge for short. She let me drape Didge around my neck for **new thing 42**. The feeling of the cold scales gave me the heebie-jeebies. Turns out I like giant lizards about as much as I like swimming with sharks and feeding lions. Large animals and reptiles unleash my old nemesis, the Imp of the Scaredy-cat. I had earlier hoped that I would summon enough courage during my year of new things to get close to the one creature that frightens me more than any other, the dastardly prickled beast that is the hedgehog. Given how I reacted to Didge the lizard, though, I doubt I ever will. I didn't enjoy wearing a live lizard as a scaly, cold scarf, but it nonetheless gave me an insight into someone I saw every day but barely knew. That, I decided, was pretty cool.

For **new thing 43** I went go-karting. About halfway through my year of new things someone pointed out how boring many of my new things were, and asked how it was that I hadn't done them already? I honestly don't know. Go-karting was one of those things. I guess I'd never been in a situation where someone else had organised it, and never cared enough to arrange it myself. I didn't suggest it or arrange it but it sounded fun, I thought. I'll jump on the go-kart bandwagon. Why not? I went with a handful of other people and was lapped by every single one of them.

Go-karting was fun: I liked wearing a giant pink helmet, as well as the odd moment when I drove faster than a sloth-snail hybrid on wheels. I especially liked the insights into the people I was with, such as that the fastest, most aggressive driver was also the quietest person of the group. Underneath the calm, she was the Usain Bolt of the go-kart track. And she also learned something about me: that I am such a slow go-karter, that, if it had been on the open road, I would have been pulled over for holding up traffic.

Another new thing I'd never have thought of myself was **new thing 44**, doing an escape vault. I had heard that escape vaults, also known as escape rooms, put otherwise civilised people into a situation where they arrive as friends and leave vowing not to speak to each other until the End of Days. My sister suggested it. In fact, she suggested we have two teams—one of my three sisters and me, then another of our partners, to see which team could escape from the room the fastest. I wasn't sure that was a good idea. There are many Christmases and birthdays and other family events between now and the End of Days that we will all be at together. It would be most inconvenient to not be on speaking terms with the person seated closest to the salt when you need it passed to you. Then, a friend also suggested doing an escape vault. As I couldn't think of any occasions in the foreseeable future when I would need to ask her to pass me a condiment, I said sure. Two other friends were keen, so off we went to an underground lair to get locked behind a safe door. The room was filled with what can best be described as Random Weird Shit, some of it glowing, which was apparently the 'clues' to help us escape. A glowing clock counted down from 60 minutes, so we had only an hour to use all our wiles and cunning to once again taste freedom.

I saw a different side to my friends in that room. It was surprising how quickly a hierarchy formed regarding who were the credible decision-makers (not me) and who were the minions (me). One friend was methodical and clever. One was very funny. One took control when we got in a flap. And one had a poor attention span and made dumb jokes about the glowing skull key. Okay, that last one was me. I suppose my friends got to see a different side of me as well. We got out eventually. Sure, we needed a twenty-minute extension and a few clues over the intercom, but that's just a minor detail, right? Intellectual problem-solving prowess is overrated. We're still talking to each other, and that's more important.

It was hard to put myself out there. I felt exposed. It's not easy to ask people to do things with you, especially unusual things. You have to constantly ignore the little voice inside your head that says, 'No one likes you because you're a dick and everyone thinks you're weird.' I get social anxiety. When I left my last job, I didn't even have a proper farewell drink, as is custom. I told everyone that it was because I had other plans, but I was just scared no one would come. But I was never going to get other people to do new things with me if I didn't ask. So I did. And sometimes the act of asking put me further out of my comfort zone than the thing I wanted to do in the first place.

I thought it would get easier as the year went on, but it didn't. You'll remember that **new thing 18** was starting a Netflix and wine group. It was genius, I thought. I love wine. I love Netflix. Why not combine them and make a club so I could call wine-drinking and TV-watching a legit hobby? Perfect! Plus, I'd been feeling a little lonely again; I needed things to connect me to other people during the week. I needed some more of the regular unplanned interactions that sociologists say are a prerequisite for making friends. I put a post on Facebook asking if anyone wanted to join. Then I waited. If no one 'liked' my post, I would feel like the biggest idiot. This is a thing, nowadays. Will people 'like' my posts or not? This question is a whole new form of possible social rejection that can haunt you everywhere you go with your phone, which is pretty much everywhere if you're like I was before my year of new things. This haunting also includes your safe spaces, where you should be feeling all warm and fuzzy, not like Loser McNomates. Places like your living room, or in the bath, or lying in bed. It sounds so lame, but it makes sense in psychological terms if you're a social-media fiend. Studies show that having people 'like' your stuff makes you feel supported.[14] Another 2014 study said that 44 per cent of Facebook users 'like' things on Facebook at least once a day, 29 per cent more than once a day[15]. No wonder not getting any likes feels a bit shit. You know people are there, scrolling past your post. We can blame the algorithms all we like (which, granted, do work against us sometimes), but when you're not feeling particularly resilient, not being 'liked' feels like the modern-day equivalent of someone seeing you coming and crossing to the other side of the street. But worse, because you're not in the street. You're everywhere, and everybody else can see.

So, there I was, with my wine and Netflix post. After five minutes, nobody had 'liked' it, so I lost my nerve and took the post down. It was a stupid idea anyway, I thought. I moped around for a while, before sitting back at the computer and glaring at the screen. Eventually I summoned the courage to repost the message and forced myself not to look again until the next day. Social affirmation shouldn't matter that much; rational me knows this. But when I'm not feeling good, my rational mind has gone to somewhere gloomy for a holiday in the rain. I imagined my Facebook friends rolling their eyes in unison. In my mind, they said the same things as my inner voice: *I don't even like her. She's such a dick. Why would I want to join some weird club?* Yet, when I checked the next morning, I was glad I'd gone out on a limb. So glad. People were interested. Not just any people, but random people, some of whom I hadn't seen in years. Inner voice be damned. It didn't know what it was talking about. I was fine. My best friend from school got in touch too, all the way from mainland USA. She was far away, but still wanted to join. So did another old school friend in Denmark, then another in the UK, and another in Australia.

So, I started a virtual wine and Netflix group. We invited some other girls from school and we talked about what television we were watching. It was lovely to talk about minutiae with them again. Liking their posts online was nothing compared to agreeing to watch the same shows from our different time zones and having a natter about it. Other people joined the Facebook group, people I didn't know. The group is still going, with about 70 members, and I post regularly. Usually on a Friday or Saturday evening when I'm home alone and want recommendations of what to watch. I've never been disappointed. And it makes me feel less alone. I may be sitting watching television in an empty house, but I'm still part of a community.

While the year of new things did help lessen my feelings of loneliness, it wasn't the magic bullet I had hoped it would be. Loneliness is a hard problem to solve; it's too tenacious and dastardly. People's suggestions showed me more about who they were, I got back in touch with some old friends and found an online community. But those people were the exception. Most people weren't interested.

At the beginning, during my Sam-I-Am frenzy, people agreed to all sorts of things. I was told 'yes' much more than I was told 'no'. Old friends jumped at the idea of new things, emailing through suggestions, telling me about all of the things we could do together. I got excited about all of these new experiences I could have with people who I wanted to reconnect with. I didn't know how I'd fit in all of these ideas coming at me from all directions, but I couldn't wait to find out. *Oh, the fun I will have with all of these people in my life! I will not be lonely any longer,* I thought. But my purple notebook was filled with ideas that didn't go anywhere.

Most people will agree to almost anything if it's presented to them enthusiastically. Some people really did want to do the things at some indeterminate time in the future that never actually happens. Some were just humouring me. Some probably just didn't want to say no to the lady who looked like she was cracking under the surface. Or they were like me and being a life model: they liked the idea, not the reality (more on that later). I get that. It's fine. It's hard to say no to someone, especially if you're a hard-wired people-pleaser. We also live in a culture where directly refusing an offer can feel like we're being rude or unpleasant, so we say yes and hope it will never come to pass.

As I said earlier, yes is the new maybe, and maybe is the new no. As the months passed, the old script started to replay itself. People wanted to do things in the abstract, but were hard to pin down. Or they were only available when I was busy. Or we would agree to something and one of us would get sick. Or they would hook up with a man from work and spend the day we'd made plans engaged in a shag-a-thon of epic proportions instead. I didn't hold it against them; this is how life rolls. And, regarding the shag-a-thon friend, I had nothing but envy, although we never did manage to reschedule the geocaching we'd planned to do. (I still don't actually know what geocaching is, although my shag-a-thon friend tells me it is a good way to spend an afternoon when one is not otherwise occupied.)

But I only had 52 weeks. If I waited until that magic moment when my calendar and the calendars of people with equally busy lives lined up, I'd need 52 years. If my new things were going to fix my loneliness, I needed to build my own self-esteem and enjoy my own company again. I needed to do things alone.

Doing things alone rather than with friends is scarier and requires more motivation, especially if it's something that other people usually do in company. There is no one to remember the experience with, and you don't get any photos of yourself that aren't either a selfie or one of those awkward taken-by-a-stranger pics. I hate those. I feel daft posing in those ones, so I just stand uncomfortably, with a look in my eye that says, 'Please don't run away with my camera.' When by yourself, you're not accountable to anyone else, so if it's something that's pushing you outside of your comfort zone, it's easier to back out.

Being alone can also be awkward. I felt painfully self-conscious waiting for my helicopter ride, **new thing 15**, which I mentioned in an earlier chapter. All of the other passengers were a family having an adventure for their dad's sixty-fifth. I felt like the sixth wheel, especially when one charming specimen of good breeding rolled his eyes and said to his sister: 'Is *she* coming too?' For **new thing 45** I went to a political meet-the-candidates evening. It's the sort of thing I'd been meaning to do for years: taking the chance to actually hear from the people on the ballot before deciding which box to tick. I wanted to hear from them all in person, without their messages being filtered by the media. I asked around: does anyone want to join me? But everyone was busy. In the spirit of my year of new things, I went anyway.

When I arrived I slunk into the back row. I was suffering from the 'spotlight effect', which I talked about in my chapter on my looks—that feeling that everyone is watching your every move, when in truth they probably don't notice you at all.[16]

**New thing 46**, parasailing, was something else I did alone. Parasailing! Screw you, Imp of the Scaredy-cat! I had visions of sailing through the air like a bird, a majestic bird: an eagle or an albatross. Not a manky scavenger bird, that avian sky-rat the seagull. Parasailing is set up for people to do in pairs. It's not only cheaper to do it with someone else, but expected. When I asked the man operating the boat whether many people did it alone, he shrugged.

'No,' he said. 'It's an experience to be shared, I think.'

As I sat on the back of boat and waited for the wind to carry me upward, I wished I had someone sitting beside me. I felt very alone, like a lonely bird. A pair of seagulls sat together on the dock. Maybe it would have been better to be a seagull in a pair than a lone albatross. Four separate people had said they'd go parasailing with me, yet here I was. Sitting in a strange and uncomfortable seat. Alone.

**New thing 47**, going to a music festival by myself, was also deeply uncomfortable. I'd wanted to go to WOMAD for years, but had never been able to get a group together. I thought it was time to put on my big-girl pants and go anyway, so booked a ticket. The shame of being alone still hung around me like a black cloud, though. My confidence was growing as the year went on, but there was still that little voice in my head that whispered 'Loser.' What sort of person goes to a music festival alone? The night beforehand I lay in bed and regretted my decision to go. It felt weird and awkward and uncool. Music festivals are made for people to attend in gaggles, not as a lone wolf.

And yet, each time I did something alone, the experience was somehow enriched. The helicopter pilot took pity on me and sat me in the best seat. During the parasailing, as soon as I was up in the air, I was pleased to be by myself. If I'd been with someone else, I would have chattered nervously. I would have cracked bad jokes about funeral songs and drowning. I wouldn't have sat in complete silence and felt a rare sense of inner peace wash over me. And, as for the music festival, it didn't even matter I'd gone alone. There were plenty of people I knew there, including my cousin, my next-door neighbour and an old school teacher. I ended up spending most of the festival with an old university friend I hadn't seen in years. It wasn't until I saw her that I realised how much we had to catch up on. We sat in the sun and talked and talked and listened to music and talked some more. There is something so grounding about seeing old friends. You have known so many iterations of each other, yet you remain drawn to the essence of who they are, and they you. Even if you don't have much in common day to day, when you share history, it doesn't matter. Then, contact begets contact. If I hadn't seen her at the festival, she would possibly still be someone who I would think about every now and again, and think *I must drop her a line sometime*, but never do.

So here I was, learning more about the people I already knew, and getting more confident about doing things alone. I wanted to do something else to put my loneliness in perspective, so for **new thing 48**, I volunteered at a retirement village.

'Talk to the residents,' the nurse said. 'It doesn't matter what you talk about. Just talk to them.'

The retirement village was confronting. Mum worked at a retirement village when I was a kid. I remember it being a smelly place filled with people who frightened me, including a resident who used to tell Mum she looked like a 'moo cow'. But I was a kid. I might have been frightened of the moo-cow lady, but at that time I also thought there was no achievement nobler than being able to eat a piece of dry Weet-Bix faster than my sister. I was a grown-up now. I thought it would be easy to volunteer. It wasn't. Some of the residents were very old, very sick or both. Being there was the most emotionally intense of all my new things. Which is saying something, as I did relationship counselling, after all.

Old age is stigmatised. It makes no sense on a rational level: most people want to reach old age and to die, elderly, in their beds à la Rose from *Titanic*. We don't want to be taken young, like Jack from *Titanic* after Rose didn't share the floating door. Why then is seeing the very elderly so confronting at times? Maybe it does make sense on a rational level. Maybe it's uncomfortable because we know we're looking into a mirror and seeing where we might ourselves be within the blink of an eye.

'I'm going to see my mum today,' one resident said. 'I can't wait.'

I did my math: her mum would have passed away at least thirty years earlier, maybe more.

'Good for you,' I said.

Some of the residents were heartbreakingly lonely. Many elderly people are. I left the retirement home acutely aware of how lucky I am. While I get lonely, I am still young enough and physically able enough to seek out company. I do not sit in a communal living room, hoping that one of the volunteers will join me in doing a puzzle. I can still visit my own mum, even if her stomach cancer has meant that we won't be eating vodka-infused doughnuts again, like we did for **new thing 34**. Indeed, I am lucky. Very lucky.

It's not just about age. While it's hard to make friends when you're past your twenties, it's even harder for some. Sometimes I feel dorky and awkward with people I don't know, like my tongue is swollen and everything that falls out of my mouth is verbal diarrhoea. But I'm fortunate not to have crippling shyness. I am privileged because I have the physical ability to leave the house, and the mental and material resources to do the things I've done. I'm also lucky that I didn't go under: my Downward Spiral of Suck had a ladder out. Some people live in their Downward Spiral of Suck for months or even years. For there are some issues that parasailing, riding in a helicopter and wearing bright red lipstick won't fix.

By this point I'd done fifteen activities completely alone and there were a further five that I'd expected to do alone but had people join me once I'd locked them in. Each time, I felt better about my own company, as each activity I did alone was a reminder that I could do it. As my confidence grew, I started doing more and more things to strengthen my connections with other people. Things that had nothing to do with my new things but made me feel so much better: attending parties alone, joining a new book club and saying 'yes' rather than 'maybe' to events with people I hadn't seen in a while and then actually turning up. I felt like I had friends again.

Of course, I still have my moments. This isn't a feel-good movie. Loneliness, like unhappiness, is a giant rubber hand that can come out of nowhere and slap you around the face at any time. The challenge isn't keeping it away forever—for some of us, that might be impossible. To even attempt such a thing would be to live with a constant sense of failure, making you feel bad when you are already down. No, the challenge is to minimise the sting of the slap, and throw the hand back in the closet before it can slap you on the other cheek as well. The challenge is to stretch out the time between slaps, and to make them sting less.

My challenge is to always remember that I may sometimes feel lonely standing in a crowd, but I'm pretty bloody lucky to have the resources to reach out to the crowd around me, which I now know I can do.

And, I think, being aware of that is good progress indeed.

# 9

# A CIRCULAR
# LINE TO DOING
# NOT MUCH

※ **New thing 49**: Doing a DNA test

**AS DR EDITH EGER WROTE IN** her memoir, *The Choice*, 'no one heals in a straight line'.[1]

We think we ought to, but we don't. You stride confidently from our dark place to your happy ending, but right at the point when you get cosy and think life is good again, something happens and you find yourself stuck in the brambles by the side of the road. Then, when you eventually find yourself back on the road, it's not the same place you fell off. You've got some new cuts, and you're even further back from your happiness nirvana. Healing and building self-esteem is a long, complicated process that takes time and self-care. That's why I think of healing as being like the needle on one of those old sets of scales, a needle that moves up and down then up and down some more before eventually settling on a number. Our needles always go up and down as we have good days and bad days, but it's the default setting that matters. It's not about being good all of the time. It's about the good days being a bit better and the bad days being not quite so bad.

During my year of new things, my default needle crept higher and higher as the foundations for my resilience were restored. By the time the next winter rolled around, I felt much better. I was body-confident. I had better support networks and healthier friendships. Alan and I had a stronger relationship than we'd had for years. Not going out for 'a few drinks and a bit of banter' was better for my health, both physical and mental. Best of all, I had more emotional energy for Jack and Dahla: during my year of new things, I'd learned to fit my own oxygen mask, so I could give myself more to my parenting. The year pulled me out of a black hole, and taught me about myself and the people around me. Planning things gave me back the focus I'd been lacking, and also something fun to think about when I found myself getting lost in the caverns of my mind.

Yet, no one heals in a straight line.

My year of new things was drawing to a close when I fell back off the road and got tangled up in a bramble bush. My lovely nephew died. He was only three. After that, things got hard. The weather turned; it was cold and wet. Little things chipped away at my resilience: an unexpected bill; getting caught in the rain wearing a dress that remained sodden for hours; getting regular nosebleeds that stained the carpet and left the bathroom looking like a scene from a horror movie. The sort of things that are totally manageable on their own, but that seem insurmountable when they happen all at once. The Downward Spiral of Suck orbited in my peripheral vision. I kept it together: walking forward; planning new things; doing fun things with Alan and the children; and doing things that usually made me feel better.

One cold winter's evening, I got a massage. Massage isn't something I do often; I love them, but there seems something so ridiculously decadent about paying so much money for someone to rub oils into your skin. It feels as though it's so fancy you ought to be draped on a chaise longue and be hand-fed grapes. But things had been tough, and a massage was the perfect treat. I had looked forward to it all afternoon. While lying on that bed I felt happy, grapes or no grapes. When I groggily sat up after the masseuse was done, even my fingertips were relaxed. Ahhh. As I wrapped up warm, I thought: *That was worth the money.* I stepped out into the darkness and walked down the street toward my bus, still all warm on the inside in that feel-good way that's impossible to write about without sounding cornier than a Kansas cornfield.

Then: the friend I'd had the falling out with over social media, standing in front of me. My former friend who would ask me if I was dead when I didn't reply to her messages quickly enough. My former friend who used me for emotional support for years, all the while reciprocating only when it suited her and was on her terms.

I hadn't seen her in months, and there she was, right where I was about to walk. I hadn't thought about her for a while. As time passed and I'd healed from the situation, she'd slowly slipped from my mind. The hole she'd left in my life had been filled by other friends and much healthier friendships.

I did a quick assessment of the situation in the manner inherited from our cave-dwelling ancestors. What were my options to avoid awkwardness? I didn't have many. If I stopped walking mid-stride and turned around and she'd already seen me, I'd look like a dick. Swivelling in another direction would look equally obvious. Walking past and pretending not to see her was also an option, and the thing I'd always imagined I'd do. Although, in my imagination, it would be sunny, I wouldn't be huddled under a giant coat, and I wouldn't have massage oil in my hair. Isn't that what we always hope will happen? Breeze past, looking happy and awesome? But this was my friend, who I realised at that moment I'd really missed. So I stopped. *It'll be fine*, I thought. *We'll swap a few pleasantries and have a laugh. I've got this.* I said hello. She looked me in the eye, turned her back on me and walked away.

The next morning I woke shrouded in a deep sense of loss I couldn't quite place. Some days, the shroud never came off. I felt disappointed in my own brain for not being able to think its way out of this corner. After all, wasn't that what my year of new things was supposed to be for? How is it that I could come so close to the end of my year of new things and feel like this?

After some weeks had passed, I asked myself what the difference was between being glum, sad and lonely, and actually being depressed. At what point is it time to acknowledge that the best way forward comes in the form of pills? I'd never taken them before, for no reason other than having been blessed with brain chemistry that's meant I've never needed to.[2] I'm open to the idea of antidepressants or anti-anxiety medication. Many people I know take them—more than I can count off the top of my head—and that's just the people I'm close enough to for them to tell me about it. As the stigma around mental health slowly lifts, more and more people talk openly about their own battles. But we still don't actually know how many people suffer, as it's chronically under-reported. According to the longitudinal study of children born in Dunedin during 1972 and 1973, mental illness is twice as high as mental-health professionals have been led to believe.[3] Many people simply don't tell others when the black dog comes barking, and certainly not record-keepers. And, if people don't speak up, it's impossible to get a full and accurate picture of how many people wear shrouds of doom. What we do know, however, is that mental-health issues are far-reaching. So many people take antidepressants, waterways in Western cities contain traces of them.[4] Even during my winter of new things, my sadness and loneliness had never reached a critical point for a sustained period of time. Was this time different?

With this knowledge came a whole new wave of despair, as well as sad frustration. I'd spent most of the year doing everything I was supposed to do, but still felt low. Maybe I was more broken than a few dollops of superglue in the form of new things could fix? I'd always been a tad anxious and, to quote Johann Hari in his book on depression, depression and anxiety are 'like cover versions of the same song by different bands'.[5] It was reasonable to think that I'd jumped from one song cover to the other. Studies also show that depression is 37 per cent inherited, with the rest down to environment. So, while someone might possess the switch of depression, it's often down to their circumstances whether or not that switch is flicked.[6] Had my recent experiences flicked my switch?

One sunny Sunday afternoon, I started to cry. I'm not a big crier, not really. The times I've mentioned crying in this book are the only times I'd cried in the previous year, and these were tears of the silently-pouring-down-your-cheeks-for-a-short-period variety. That Sunday was a whole different league of crying: wailing, ugly face-contortions and an inability to stay upright. It was the sort of crying that people mock in the movies. There was no specific trigger; I was walking across a bridge near my house, and the tears started to flow. I cried the whole way home and then continued, without exaggeration, for the next hour. It was lucky no one was there.

I cried about my nephew dying, and cried because my kids were so sad about losing him too and I couldn't do anything to help them. I then cried because it was a beautiful day and I was still sad. I cried because I felt like I had done everything in my power over the previous year to feel my very best, but still felt as though I had failed. Then I cried because I had a headache from crying so much. After I'd finished I went to bed, even though it was only 3 p.m., and went to sleep.

After that, things felt different. It was like a giant balloon that had been blown up too much so was straining and straining and had finally popped. The pain had morphed into tears and seeped out my eyes, and it didn't feel quite so raw anymore. I'll be sad about my nephew for the rest of my life, but, I knew I could find a way to coexist with the pain. My head throbbed from crying and my eyes were red and sore, but I thought, *I got this. I really do have this. Life will be fine. I'm going to be okay.*

My needle had dropped to a low point, but now it was being pulled back to somewhere closer to its default position. My year of growth and change had counted for something after all. I still had bad spells, thanks to that un-straight line of healing, but life was much better than it had been when I started. I had more confidence. I'd had fun. I looked better as my acne had cleared and I had more tools to improve my appearance, but, paradoxically, I cared much less. I'd reconnected with old friends, made new ones and felt better socially than I had before. My parenting had improved as I had more mental energy for the children, and more focus. My self-esteem was so much higher as a result. And, best of all, I had Alan and the children. Lovely, reliable, kind Alan. How lucky I was to come through the year and have Alan there for me when I needed him. How lucky I was that he was still part of my script. I didn't care what the next chapters of my script looked like, as long as my family were in it.

Then, something odd happened. I had four more things to do. Only four! There were more than four things I wanted to try; I'd need a decade to finish all of the things on the list in my purple notebook. But I simply didn't care anymore. I'd signed up for an obstacle course through mud, but when it rolled around I chose to take Dahla to a birthday party instead. I signed up for a superhero run with the kids and bought us all cheap Superman capes to wear, but we were all tired that morning, so stayed home and watched a movie. One evening Alan and I had a babysitter, but instead of doing something new and exciting to get the fear-juices flowing, we drove to the beach, looked out to sea and talked. It was winter again, but now I was finding the quiet life nice, not lonely. Rather than being out and about doing new things, I wanted to read, see friends and watch television. For the most part, time in my own company felt like solitude rather than loneliness. I'd talked to people about going back to Adrenalin Forest at the end of my year, but found myself wanting to binge-watch television instead.

The only new thing I did during this period was **new thing 49**, a DNA test, which Mum had given me as a gift the previous Christmas. I was curious about my DNA make-up, but also suspicious. Like many people of Māori origin (especially those of us with white faces), the question of 'Just how Māori *are* you exactly?' has been asked many times in my life and often in a way that has made me feel uncomfortable. I wasn't completely sure I wanted to know. At least I'd been given it by Mum, so that probably meant that I wasn't going to find out that my dad was actually the milkman or some other surprise of that ilk.

It was a cool gift, so I spat in the tube and sent it off to Ireland. The results were roughly the same general mix of ethnicities I had expected, albeit with a much higher dose of Scandinavian blood than previously thought. Perhaps that explains my love for Swedish car-shaped candy. And at least now I have a ready answer when interrogated about my blood quantum, and know for sure that I am not the secret spawn of the local milkman.

I was out of ideas, though. I was stuck at 49 new things and running out of time. I wanted to stop. I was tired. I'd totally run out of steam and imagination. But I couldn't stop. Not at this point. If I stopped with only three new things to go, I would be disappointed in myself. There were still things to do, including the scariest thing of all.

# 10

## THE BEST
## JOKE IN
## THE ROOM

※ **New thing 50**: Doing an overnight hike

※ **New thing 51**: Entering a public dance competition

※ **New thing 52**: Performing stand-up comedy

**THOUGH I DON'T MIND LAUGHING AT** myself, I'm terrified of looking like a dick in public. I'm especially scared of being laughed at. Is that normal? I suppose it is. No one wants to look like a fool in front of other people. Embarrassment cuts deep, and hangs around for decades. When I was eleven, I was standing in class when the Velcro on my skirt came loose and my skirt fell down around my ankles. The name of the teacher I had that year eludes me, but I remember that moment so well I could do a live-action reenactment: who was there, where we were standing, the weather that day. Not to mention the colour of my underwear (yellow) and the laughter of my classmates (loud and overflowing with schadenfreude). That stuff loiters for a lifetime. With memories like that echoing around our souls, it's little wonder that the fear of exposing ourselves to ridicule feels hard-wired in our brains.

Some people seem to find a way to overcome that fear. They either genuinely don't care what people think, or they keep their fear of embarrassment well-hidden. They do their thing without fear of being laughed at. If there's laughing to be done, it's not at them, but with them. These people seem so confident and brave. Because they are brave, they stand tall and unapologetic, and, by some sort of voodoo, their self-assurance renders them even more awesome. I wanted to be like those people. I *needed* to be like those people. After a few instances of feeling uncomfortable in public settings or not putting myself forward for things that involved being in front of others, I realised that my fear of being laughed at in public was holding me back. I've trained to do earnest public speaking about factual things, but anything personal or funny? No way. I felt awkward, shy and nervous sharing myself like that. This fear made me not want to do certain things in front of others if I could help it, especially high-profile things. I've long dreamed of doing something big and cool like a TEDx Talk, but that was never going to happen if I kept avoiding a certain type of public speaking because I was scared the audience would laugh at me. I wanted this fear to go away, but I didn't quite know how to make it happen.

Given I was terrified of being laughed at by random strangers, I laughed at myself an awful lot. The ability to laugh at yourself is a strange thing. Some people are better at it than others. I can think of a few people I know who are so deadly serious about life they stray as close to imitating the Dementors of Azkaban as is humanly possible. They could slip on a stray banana peel while running to the Benny Hill chase theme, and you still couldn't so much as smile—you wouldn't dare. If you did, you would require the same Benny Hill chase theme as you ran away from their Dementor-wrath.

I heard a quote once about how if you can't laugh at yourself, you might be missing the best joke in the room. I liked that quote. Maybe I *was* the best joke in the room? I might as well laugh, then; what a shame it would be to miss out on that.

Humour as a coping mechanism makes sense from a

psychological perspective—to quote Abraham Lincoln: 'I laugh because I must not cry.' Besides, I love laughing, especially at the sort of quick-fire banter that makes your sides ache. I don't mean the laugh I give when Jack and Dahla tell me for the tenth time in nine minutes that cows love to go to the Moooseum. I'm certainly not talking about what I call Lame Loser Laughter. You know the sort of laughter I mean: the half-laugh you give when everyone else is laughing at a joke you don't get, when you know you can't laugh too hard just in case the joke is at your expense. Lame Loser Laughter is that weird laugh we give when someone has told a tremendously bad joke, but the moment is so awkward we laugh to make the moment go away. The worst kind of Lame Loser Laughter is the laugh we give when someone has said something offensive and everyone knows it's not quite right but no one is brave enough to call it out. No, that's not the sort of laughing I love. The kind of laughter I love is loud, shameless laughter that can sometimes accidentally sound like a seal barking and make you cry. People who make you laugh like that are more precious than the blingiest bling, and ought to be valued as such.

For years, my personal mantra was 'It's either a good time or a good story.' I believed this to be true for almost everything, with a few exceptions: long waits in airport lounges, burning your toast, parking tickets, and—of course—legit nasty and horrible things. Some really good comedy comes from pain. It's what Golden Globe-winning actor and co-creator of the excellent show *Crazy Ex-Girlfriend* Rachel Bloom calls 'fuck you through the tears'.[1] When bad things happened to me or times were tough, I would look to find the funny story hiding within. Life might suck, but I didn't want to risk missing out on the best joke in the room. Abraham Lincoln had the right idea. Laughing was so much better than crying.

This was especially true doing **new thing 50**, an overnight hike. I'd been picturing the hike for weeks in advance: a lovely walk; three friends; reading a book in the sun; communing with nature. I bought a new T-shirt to wear (red, practical and flattering!) and thought hard about which book would make the communing-with-nature experience complete. Of course I couldn't choose between two, so I took them both. When can one have too many books? Never!

The trek to the hut started out as I'd expected—a nice meander on a proper path. Little did I know then that the path would disappear after about a kilometre. The rest of the walk would be less walking and more scrambling over tree roots and stones and wading through giant puddles. It was hard work, especially while wearing a heavy pack, and I had stupidly packed the books instead of a second, dry, pair of shoes. When can one have too many books? When they are heavy and take up too much backpack space. As much as I love books, I couldn't wear them on my feet while taking a midnight stroll to the smelly outdoor long drop. I also had blisters the size of Jupiter's moons. One of my friends lent me his shoes to wear so I could go outside while my hiking boots were still sodden.

'If your blisters pop while you're wearing my shoes, I'm never speaking to you again,' he said.

It was cold up there in the hills. Very cold. I wore the new red T-shirt I'd bought specially, but it was hidden under two layers of polypropylene and that item of clothing that has now become a supporting character in this book, 'The Scab'. It was also too cold to read outside. I tried, but it rained on me. Then it got dark and all we had were head torches so reading wasn't much fun anyway.

The next day, there was no one in the hut except my wee group and a man we didn't know. The man didn't have any hiking gear, and looked like someone who actually lived in the hills. He was keen to chat. I put on my best listening face as he told his story of being screwed over by 'the Man', without specifying who 'the Man' was or how 'the Man' had executed his dastardly life-screwing plan.

Then he pulled out a gun.

I have never felt so far from civilisation in my life. We hadn't had mobile reception for over 24 hours, and it was at least a five-hour walk back to the car. Could we run? Perhaps. Me and my moon-sized blisters wouldn't be able to move very quickly. My boots were still wet, and my books hadn't magically transformed into alternative footwear overnight. Books are annoying like that.

The man stood on the balcony and started taking random shots into the distance.

'I love shooting out here in the wilderness,' he said. 'Bang, bang, bang!'

We left as quickly as we could, me in my wet boots. Nothing like a man with a gun to give you a dose of motivation. Then, about an hour later, while lost, we were caught in a downpour.

I sat in the rain and thought I saw the man with the gun in every shadow, ready to take a shot in my direction. Once we finally found the track again, it was a long walk out. Every step hurt and I had to walk like John Wayne to minimise the thigh chaffage. Eventually we were there. Hurrah! I hobbled towards the car. Never before had the idea of sinking into a soft seat been more inviting. Of course it wasn't that easy. The soft seat was covered in glass, for some paragon of goodness and virtue had smashed the car window while we'd been in the hills. They had also stolen my friend's clothes as well as a bag of corn chips. It was a long drive home that evening, in a car with a missing window.

But I still managed to laugh. I had to. If I hadn't laughed, I would have shaken my fist at the sky instead and wailed like a banshee. Laughing was much better, not to mention far less melodramatic.

'Maybe it was the man with the gun that broke into the car,' my friend said. 'All that shooting makes a man hungry for corn chips.'

'Why didn't they steal my clothes?' the other friend said. 'Are they trying to tell me I'm not fashionable?'

'Maybe corn chips are his gift for "The Man",' said the third friend.

I was so glad to be with people who also prefer to laugh than cry. When I think back to that hike, it's not the bad stuff I think about. It's all the laughing, being in nature and the lovely, restful feeling of being in the middle of nowhere. There are many times when the ability to laugh at yourself is a good trait to have. I'd do the walk again if the chance arose, albeit with more of those snazzy gel Band-Aids that are supposed to prevent blisters, and no books. And, perhaps, a bulletproof vest.

When it comes to laughing at myself, I've got a wee collection of anecdotes and stories I've nursed over the years. One is my fear of hedgehogs. It was my go-to for those naff team-building activities in which everyone must share a 'fun fact' about themselves. I hope for your sake you have never endured the awkwardness that is sharing 'fun facts' with colleagues. You don't want your factoids to be dull, too show-offy or risqué, and there is a very fine line between those three things. One workmate said that they had once skied completely naked. It is a fact that thinking about this was not, indeed, fun. Hedgehogs are no nude skiing, but it is something I can laugh about. Besides, I think it's a perfectly rational fear. How can something be covered in spikes and *not* be the spawn of Satan? Hedgehogs don't even walk properly. They scuttle about in a way which suggests all manner of evil brewing in their spike-covered heads. It's no coincidence that 'hedgehog' rhymes with 'Lucifer-og'. Hedgehogs are the Voldemort of the undergrowth. People often laugh at my fear of hedgehogs. I am regularly sent photos of them and gifted with hedgehog paraphernalia. My sister gave Jack a toy hedgehog when he was born. I named it Beelzebub, not expecting it to become Jack's favourite toy. One day when he was four he took it to day care. The teacher wanted to talk to me at pickup.

'Jack says his toy is called Beelzebub,' she said. 'That's not right, is it?'

'Ahhhh,' I said. 'Well, actually, that's its name. Beelzebub.'

The teacher raised her eyebrows. 'Perhaps we should just call it Beezy when it's here then?'

I laughed awkwardly. This was even more embarrassing than the time Jack had asked a random man on the bus if he had a penis. Ever since then, Beelzebub has been an 'at-home' toy. I said it was because he's so special, we wouldn't want to lose him, but you and I both know the truth: to avoid more such awkward moments.

One of my other stories is about porn. When I was at university, back in the pre-wifi dark ages, I had a boyfriend. This former boyfriend and I had been together about a year when the idea of watching porn came up. Porn! I'd never seen porn before. Not properly, anyway. Things were different then, unlike now when—depressingly—most pre-teens have seen porn in some way, shape or form. A nineteen-year-old who hasn't seen porn nowadays would be as rare as a sabre-toothed tiger flying a plane. Not so back then. In the university hall of residence in first year, someone hired a porno on VHS. About twenty of us watched it together in the communal TV lounge, making jokes about quivering love puddings and giggling. I couldn't really see the screen though as I was seated too far back, and the TV was tiny, as TVs often were back then. So the following year, when my boyfriend suggested it, I said sure. It wasn't a sexy-time thing; rather, we were curious. And who wouldn't be? So off we went to the local video library to try to slip in as incognito as possible and select something to watch.

Who remembers the porn section of video libraries back in the day when we still had video libraries? The rude section was usually in a corner, and always behind a curtain. My sisters and I used to call it the 'pink' section. Why? Because once, when we sneaked behind the curtain as kids, we were overwhelmed by pinkness. My eyes almost popped out of my young head at the sight of all of the ample bosoms. I still remember how precariously one lady was perched on a motorcycle, and was concerned that she would topple off. Her large hair and her even larger bust would really have messed with her centre of gravity. We weren't supposed to be in the pink section, and we knew we'd been naughty. Afterward, I was bursting at the seams with our secret. I needed to ask one question of Mum. I knew it would betray what we'd done, but it was burning a hole in my mind.

'Mum,' I said, 'why weren't the ladies wearing normal knickers? Why did their knickers disappear up their bums?'

The pink section of the store hadn't changed much between being a kid and being nineteen: rows of videos with titles like *Good Will Humping*, *Night of the Giving Head* and *The Boobyguard*. I was too shy and embarrassed to choose, so I let my boyfriend do it. I slunk outside and loitered while he paid for the video using his own membership card. Just $8 for overnight rental!

Bargain. The video he chose was called *Easy Prey* and set in a prison. Okay, sounded interesting. We stopped at the shop to buy some chocolate ice cream as a video-watching snack and went back to my flat.

I sat in the living room, of course, because that's where the video player was, with my flatmates popping in and out to laugh. Like I said earlier, it wasn't a sexy-time thing. In fact, the video was a bit boring. There were men in outfits that didn't look prison-approved (far too holey!) and lots of dropping-the-soap. There was also something about the video that didn't feel right, but I couldn't quite put my finger on it. I looked down at my ice cream, then back at the small TV playing the VHS. The figurative penny dropped. I turned to my boyfriend.

'Where are all the women?'

I didn't know that my then boyfriend was gay. He didn't know how to tell me. And there I was, watching an $8 VHS of scantily clad men, with me realising that I was the wrong gender for my partner. I've told that story many times over the years, and always been the first to laugh. Including with my ex-boyfriend, with whom I'm still friends. He got married to his husband not long after gay marriage became legal, and I went to his wedding. He came to mine as well, and my children call him Uncle. I asked him if I could write about *Easy Prey* in here and he said that's fine as long as his mum never reads it. So, if you're reading, ex-boyfriend's mum, this book wasn't written by the Lauren you know. It's another Lauren. One that has no connection to your son whatsoever.

Indeed, I was good at laughing at myself, but still terrified of looking like a dick in public. Is that a paradox? Perhaps. Perhaps not. (Like 'ironic' and 'droll', I've never really understood how to use the word 'paradox'.) Paradox or not, I wanted to change. But how? How could I use my year of new things to confront this fear?

I was walking through central Melbourne when I happened upon a massive stage in Federation Square. There was a spontaneous dance competition occurring at that very moment and they were looking for people to join in. Could I? Would I? Should I?

No, no, no.

But it was the year of new things. I parked my shame and fear and angst and got up on that stage, bringing my new thing count to 51.

There was a moment during the dance that I still like to think about. There I was, on stage, waving my arms like a demented windmill on crack, when I caught sight of myself on the big screen. The girl on the screen looked a bit like me, but braver. She might have looked like a dick to some people, but to everyone else, she was just someone dancing. She was someone having fun. I'm no Anna Pavlova. In fact, I don't really know how to dance at all. I once lost a pair of glasses after some vigorous head-waggling motivated those glasses to fly into the ether. Needless to say, I didn't win the competition. But I didn't care. It was fun. For the rest of the day, whenever I thought about the dance, I'd laugh out loud.

I had one thing left to do. But what?

My friend Miriama had an idea. Did I want to try stand-up comedy? She'd looked into it. There was something called Raw Meat night that we could enter. We could be comedians together; the sacrificial Raw Meat to be thrown to the lions. My reaction was similar to the public dancing but a hundred thousand million times more intense. *Hell* no, no, no. I'm not exaggerating when I say the idea brought me out in a cold sweat and motivated me to stress-eat an entire bag of marshmallows. I couldn't think of anything worse than a room full of people laughing at me. I do not like green eggs and ham of the risking-public-ridicule variety. You're vulnerable, up there on stage. Public speaking is hard enough without the added pressure of being funny. People are brutal to comics that aren't hilarious. *Brutal.* We've all seen the cartoons that end with someone being pelted with rotten tomatoes. I'd read in *The Life-changing Magic of Not Giving a F\*\*k* that a stand-up comic not being funny is one of the few times that it's okay to hurt someone's feelings, as the stand-up comic 'should have feelings of steel'.[2] I do not have feelings of steel, and I didn't fancy having them hurt. I also worried about delivering my punchline and silence descending on the room, all quiet except the rustle of a lone tumbleweed blowing past me. I think I'd prefer to be pelted with rotten tomatoes. At least then you know the audience is awake.

'No,' I said to Miriama. 'I'll come and support you. But . . . no.'

Undeterred, Miriama came back after a few days. This time, she caught me in a moment of madness.

'Okay,' I said, before resisting the urge to vomit. We then roped in a third friend, Sarah. Sarah had a story involving her son getting a bar of soap stuck somewhere soap ought not go, which was deserving of a wider audience. So **new thing 52** was set in motion—confronting my fear of looking like a dick in public and performing stand-up comedy for Raw Meat Monday.

But what the hell to talk about? My life didn't feel that interesting or funny. Not enough to justify an entire stand-up sketch in any case. There were my two go-to things to laugh about, I supposed. Hedgehogs and porn. I weighed up the relative merits of each. Hedgehogs? Porn? Hedgehogs? Porn? Porn. I decided the porn story had more potential for actual lols rather than Lame Loser Laughs, and went with that. I called up my ex-boyfriend of *Easy Prey* fame and, when he said he didn't mind, scripted my routine.

I was so scared about the stand-up I couldn't focus on anything else for days beforehand. I spent the day of the event walking around the block, unable to sit still. My mind was a constant ticker of what could go wrong. It wouldn't be funny. I'd look like a dick. My skirt would fall down like when I was eleven. I'd look like a dick. No one would laugh. No, even worse. People would pity-laugh. They would pity-laugh and look at me up on stage with sympathy eyes. Me and the lone tumbleweed would be all alone and mocked for our efforts.

And did I mention I'd look like a dick?

I stood backstage and watched the acts before mine. I was directly after a guy who was only getting Lame Loser Laughter from the audience. It was painful to watch. Then he made a joke about Auschwitz. That's not funny. Sometimes Abraham Lincoln was wrong and it's more appropriate to cry than laugh. The audience agreed. This guy eventually shuffled off the stage after a one-liner about male hair removal, wearing the expression of a man who had just given up hope of being the new Chris Rock.

Then it was my turn. I closed my eyes and reminded myself of why I was there. *I got this.* I opened my eyes again, plastered a fake grin on my face and stepped on to the stage.

Performing stand-up was simply amazing. The people laughed. Not always when I intended them to, but they laughed nonetheless. There wasn't a tumbleweed, Lame Loser Laugh or rotten tomato in sight. The more people laughed, the more eloquent and confident I felt myself become. I reached the punchline, and delivered it with what felt like excellent comic timing.

'Where were all the women?'

But the people didn't really laugh. Uh-oh. This was what I'd feared! I expanded on my point.

'I didn't know my boyfriend was gay!'

Someone whooped. There was some scattered laughter. Not like minutes earlier, when the laughter had hit me in waves. I hadn't expected this reaction. I'd thought the punchline was funny, which was daft now that I think about it. It wasn't, not really. I'd only thought it was funny because of how I'd told it over the years, without ever checking back in with myself about how the story affected my own narrative. I was wrong. It was a sad story. Not just for me, but for my ex-boyfriend, who had grown up in a time when most gay nineteen-year-olds were still in the closet. Back then, I didn't know any gay people who were out. Not a single one. Many people I knew in those days have since come out, but then it was a different story. The year we'd rented that video cassette, the word 'gay' was used as a slur. The homophobic murder of Matthew Shephard had occurred the previous year. I had a male flatmate at the time who was quite the stereotypical bigot. This Neanderthal regularly ranted about how gay men made him sick (including in front of my ex-boyfriend), and had recently pushed another bloke down the stairs at a party because he thought the poor guy was acting 'gay'. I'd raised the Neanderthal's behaviour with another flatmate, who'd shrugged and said, 'Boys will be boys.' During all of the retellings of the story, I'd talked up the difference between now and then in terms of hiring a video cassette from the pink area of a video library. I'd forgotten that the world has changed in other ways too. Had my ex-boyfriend been nineteen in 2020, I'd hope that he wouldn't have been in the closet at all. The audience saw something that I hadn't been aware of myself.

There are times when it's good to laugh, because crying won't turn the books in your backpack into spare shoes or make you not-lost when you're in the middle of nowhere in the rain. But, sometimes, telling a story for comic effect makes us focus on the wrong parts. I didn't realise that this had stopped me from dealing with certain things in my own life until I watched Hannah Gadsby's Netflix special *Nanette*. It made my head burst, especially her thoughts on using trauma for laughs.

'Punchlines need trauma, because punchlines need tension and tension feeds trauma,' she says. 'You learn from the part of the story you focus on.'[3]

This had been me, too. So often, I was focusing on the wrong part of the story, and telling it in a way that didn't help me heal. Laughing at things that happen is fine if there's no underlying issue, but that's not true for things that bruise you mentally or you find hard to deal with.

I also hadn't realised that laughing was premature if I hadn't yet processed things properly, as I then risked inviting other people to poke fun of things that still either hurt me or made me uncomfortable. And, once you've laughed about something, it's hard to back up the truck, properly examine how the thing in question made you feel, and say, 'I do not find that funny.'

Like my fear of hedgehogs. I can laugh at my hedgehog fear, but I still don't like it when people laugh at me. I laughed when Jack wanted a hedgehog cake for his fifth birthday, and I had to stay up until stupid-late the night before his party turning a pile of cake, icing and chocolate fingers into something that haunts my dreams. But it was less funny when Beelzebub got stuck behind the couch at an angle that—for a minute—looked like a real hedgehog had somehow stealth-ninjaed its way inside the house. The many photos of hedgehogs I get sent are often cute, but some of them really do give me the heebie-jeebies. I'm not joking when I say hedgehogs scare me. Sometimes I feel stuck. I've let my fear become such a joke I don't know how to set boundaries around what I find okay (posed photos of cute hedgehogs dressed as Santa Claus) and what I don't (live-action pictures of hedgehogs as they go about their devilish business in nature).

Indeed, you can hinder healing when moments turn into anecdotes. You don't search for the long-lasting psychological implications of anecdotes. When making other people laugh, it's also far too easy to slip into self-deprecation. This sort of humour can backfire. Laughing at yourself can give people permission to make fun of you in return, and other people's jokes can have very pointy edges. And sometimes you can laugh about the time your ex-boyfriend got out a gay-porn video cassette when you were nineteen, without ever really addressing why it happened in the first place. Or how it made you feel. Apart from putting you off chocolate ice cream. I've never really found it appealing since.

So there I was, up on stage. I'd just delivered a punchline that might have been funny in 1999, but was straying dangerously close to Lame Loser Laughter territory in this day and age. Luckily, I had a save up my sleeve before the rotten tomatoes flew. I looped back to something I'd said earlier, and pretended it was my intended punchline all along. The audience laughed even harder than before. Phew. I grinned, and felt such a rush of happy adrenalin course through me I punched the air. Woop! I had done it. I had performed stand-up, and hadn't looked like a dick. And even if I had, I didn't care. I was having too much fun to notice. My fear wasn't going to limit me anymore.

I watch the video recording of me doing the routine sometimes, and think, *Who is this person?* The lady on the video is far too brave to be me. She's too funny. But it *is* me. Apart from legit scary stuff like natural disasters and death and trauma and hedgehogs, nothing could have been scarier than talking about porn as part of a stand-up routine. Of all of the 52 new things I have done, the stand-up was the one thing that pushed me out of my comfort zone the most. It was, and remains, the new thing I am most proud of having completed.

I still reap the benefits from having done it. I've done public speaking on a number of occasions since, and each time is easier than the last. I still get nervous, but it's a different sort of nerves. It's not paralysing anxiety—fear of looking like a fool in a way that makes my tongue fat, renders me incapable of clear articulation and reminds me of being eleven with my skirt around my ankles. It's the right sort of nerves. Adrenalin nerves, the kind that make you amped and focused, then want to punch the air when you've finished.

I've spent a lot of time thinking about my own stories since that time. Some of them aren't as funny as I'd let myself believe. They are traumatic stories; hurtful stories; things that I had laughed about as a way of not processing my pain. I don't tell those stories anymore. There have been a few uncomfortable moments when I've had to tell someone else that I don't like a certain joke, which is never easy. Especially when it's something I've put up with for years, let alone decades. Setting new boundaries with someone who has benefited from the old ones is impossible without some sort of collateral fallout in the form of awkwardness, unhappiness or excessive passive-aggressive sighing. It's worth it, though. Boundaries keep us safe. In this case, it was worth it for my self-esteem. I am happy to laugh and be the best joke in the room, but only on my terms.

Some of my stories are still funny, though. Properly funny, not laughing-to-hide-pain funny. There are also plenty of times when laughing is so much better than crying. This pleases me. After all, if I am ever to do stand-up again, I need some material to draw from. I suppose there is always the strange man in the middle of nowhere with a gun, who may or may not have broken into my friend's car to steal corn chips. Or Beelzebub the hedgehog. I may be scared of hedgehogs, but there is something about Beelzebub's decrepit form that begs to be spun into a yarn. Especially since Jack discovered the line in 'Bohemian Rhapsody' about Beelzebub having a devil put aside, to which Beelzebub the toy is now forced to do vigorous acrobatics in front of the speaker. Yes, I don't mind being the best joke in the room if that's what it's about.

Unless the room is at day care, of course, in which case his name is Beezy.

# 11

## NEW
## THING
## 53

**THE YEAR OF NEW THINGS WAS** over. It was the second of January the following year. I'd done my 52 new things in 52 weeks, but there was still something I hadn't done. Now, though, I had the chance to do it and add something else to my list. **New thing 53**, if you will.

But could I go through with it?

We all have things we hope to do and a version of ourselves we want to be: fitter, thinner, wiser, kinder, better travelled or healthier. It can be uncomfortable to be honest with yourself about what's holding you back from being that version of yourself. Some limitations are easy to understand: money, location, health. You can't do a sea swim if you live in Wisconsin, or trek on camels through the Sahara if you don't have enough petrol money to get to the next town. Some of our limitations are more complicated. They may be less obvious, but they still prevent us from achieving our hopes and dreams.

So, what are these limitations? What might be holding us back?

Some dreams are so far outside of the realm of possibility they're amusing to think about: winning an Oscar; going into space; throwing in your job to become a professional roller-coaster aficionado. We all have these dreams. I've spent at least three first-division Lotto wins in my head, tying myself in knots about where my multiple holiday homes should be located. Are France and Italy too close together to justify a villa in each? Where in South America would be the best place for a pied-à-terre? What part of the year would be best to spend in each house? These dreams are fun. They are also safe. My sister once said that if she won first-division Lotto, she'd buy me and my other sisters matching pink cars. We all loved the idea. If it actually happened, though, my sister would probably want to spend her money on other stuff when it came down to it. I'm also not sure I'd actually want to do the school run driving an overgrown marshmallow. Besides, it would be weird if all three of my sisters and I went to the same place and the parking lot was then filled with bright pink cars. Most of the enjoyment we had talking about it came from knowing deep down that it would probably never happen.

Then there is the next layer down of hopes and dreams: those that you could achieve, in theory. It would be difficult, but it could actually happen. That doesn't mean we make the dreams a reality, though. Whether it be doing an African safari, moving to the countryside or learning to play the harmonica, we all have our fantasies about the things we would do, if only.

If only what?

Continuing to nurture your hopes and dreams becomes increasingly confronting as you move through life consistently making decisions that don't enable said hopes and dreams. Not going to Paris because you don't have the means or because you're in the middle of a global pandemic is one thing, but not having the means because you bought a second car you didn't need when you were able to travel is quite another. Not learning the piano because you work a 60-hour week and have obligations the rest of the week is one thing, but not learning the piano because you are addicted to watching reruns of *The Simpsons* is a different kettle of fish entirely. I'm not judging, of course. Sometimes it's worth watching reruns of *The Simpsons* just to catch a glimpse of The Monobrow Baby. But if you really did want to learn the piano, surely you would have found the time by now? Anything's possible in the abstract, especially if it's well in the future. Not the likely future when you are just a slightly older version of your current self. A different future—a future in which you are fitter, thinner, richer and happier due to all of the lifestyle changes you'll start next month.

Feeling like anything is possible keeps us growing, changing. it keeps us optimistic. I'd rather be happily and optimistically deluded than give up hope that things can change for the better. Sometimes, though, there comes a point when you have to admit to yourself that maybe you don't actually want something as much as you thought you did. If you really did want that thing, you'd start working towards it today. If that wasn't practical, you'd start tomorrow. Not at some vague point in the future. Like my sporadic healthy-eating regimes. So often, I wait for the following Monday to start, which means eating all of the apple pies and biscuits on the Sunday, as I have to get them out of the house, right? I need to get a fix of junk before my healthy regime, right? Or I wait to start on the first of the next month, because it's cool to start things on the first, right? Those health kicks always fail. Always.

During my year of new things, the difference between what I *thought* I wanted to do and what I *actually* wanted to do became uncomfortably apparent. There are a plethora of reasons not to do something when all you have is a month or two: there is always a work project; a commitment of some description;

something else to spend money on. A year, though, is a decent amount of time. If you have the means, an entire year is more than long enough to plan and execute something that you want to do. Assuming that, deep down, you actually want to do it, and are not dreaming.

I've been guilty of dreaming before.

Every single January, I resolve to drink more water and eat fewer pies, only to conveniently forget my resolution by the time February rolls around. I've also failed at sticking to new hobbies. When Dahla was tiny, I wanted to harness my dormant domestic goddess and make her a dress. Off I went to buy a sewing machine that we couldn't really afford, some patterns and a pile of fabric. The last article of clothing I had made was for my Barbie doll during the dark recesses of the nineties, but I wasn't concerned. I thought that sewing a dress would be the perfect segue into living a life of domestic bliss in the manner of a fifties housewife as viewed through the rosiest of rose-tinted spectacles. It wasn't. By the time I admitted defeat and gave up on sewing Dahla's dress, it wouldn't have even fitted over her limbs. I liked the idea of sewing much more than I actually liked doing it.

Some of my other faux dreams were bigger, more global. I spent my twenties defining myself as someone who was going to do volunteer work abroad. I wanted to be like my step-mum, who lived in Africa for two years doing just that. I'd heard her stories, and thought it sounded amazing. I had to do it too. Volunteer work abroad was the thing I would do after I'd finished with the current phase of my life, the thing I would do next. It's hardly a plot twist of *The Sixth Sense* proportions to say that it never happened. I liked the idea of being the sort of person who would do volunteer work one day. This was different from being the sort of person who actually did it.

Why don't we do more to achieve our dreams? What are we so afraid of?

One thing that holds us back is the subconscious fear that achieving our hopes and dreams won't be what we imagined, and that the experience will be somehow lacking. Years ago, Alan and I travelled to Rome with my bestie George. When he's not making up derogatory nicknames for my grey polar fleece, George is an avid history buff who had always wanted to visit Rome. We were at the Colosseum. It was amazing (it is the Colosseum, after all), but it was also cold and wet, and we'd got lost trying to find it.

'How do you feel, being here? Is it what you always hoped?' I asked George.

'It's cool,' George said. 'But I'm hungry and I need to pee.'

Now George mentioned it, I realised that I, too, was hungry and needed to visit the facilities. The awe I'd felt at the Romans' architectural prowess was also then rudely interrupted by some men dressed as Roman soldiers trying to charge us many euros to grace us with their presence in a photo. And where *were* the bathrooms? Nowhere I could see. Not the free ones, anyway. Indeed, wanting to visit somewhere for most of your adult life doesn't insure you against getting there, being hungry and needing to pee. If we don't even attempt to do these things, then whenever we think about the thing in question, we can continue to imagine a spiritual experience with angels singing and bells clanging. Not frantically searching for a public bathroom and evading men dressed in plastic armour. Indeed, there can be an inverse relationship between how much you look forward to something and how much you enjoy it. The more you look forward to something the more pressure you put on it, so the better it has to be to meet your expectations. Much like every New Year's Eve party I've ever attended, as compared to the random unplanned evenings that turned into the stuff of legends.

Fear of failure also holds us back from achieving our goals. This is especially true for things that require any sort of skill and practice. In *Pride and Prejudice*, Lady Catherine de Bourgh says that, if she had ever learned the piano, she would have been a great proficient. That's a much nicer thought than actually learning the piano and realising you're a bit crap. Sometimes it's easier to self-sabotage. That way we can remain like Lady Catherine, convinced that, had we learned something, we would have been brilliant. As I wrote in the chapter on beauty, I'd self-sabotaged my looks for most of my adult life. I see people around me self-sabotage in other ways. They leave assignments until the last minute on purpose, so if they get a low grade, they can say it didn't matter as they only wrote it the day before. I know people who don't write the novel they have in their heads, because a great unwritten novel is better than a mediocre written one that might not get published. I see people sign up to courses to learn things they've always wanted to know, but stop turning up. The idea that failure won't hurt if you don't really try in the first place is an ingrained self-defence mechanism. It also becomes a self-fulfilling prophecy, because achieving success at most things requires at least some application.

Even realising our ambitions can be complicated. As much as achieving certain things might feel like nirvana from afar, the closer you get to your goalposts, the more likely they are to move again. Chasing the shiny doesn't always work. You can always be richer, thinner, more lauded and win more awards. Studies tracking first-division Lotto winners show a surprising amount of bankruptcy, shattered relationships and lives that later reverted back to what they were like before the win. But worse, because where there had once been some money, now there was none. This is true for other aspects of life. Desperately wanting a baby doesn't mean you won't get post-natal depression, and being conventionally 'successful' does not mean you don't suffer mental-health problems, have health issues or secretly hate your job. Some things look better from afar. Nor is conventional 'success' a magic bullet for happiness. Unless your success has been accompanied by some sort of journey of self-discovery, you're still you, regardless of how much kudos you get. Leo Tolstoy wrote *War and Peace*, a book people deliberately place in the centre of their bookshelves at eye level in order to look erudite. The sort of people who would use the word erudite on purpose, even though research shows that using long words when simple ones will do doesn't make you look very clever at all.[1] But writing *War and Peace* wasn't enough for old Tolstoy. He asked himself in *A Confession*:

'well, fine, so you will be more famous than Gogol, Pushkin, Shakespeare, Molière, more famous than all the writers in the world, and so what?'[2] You'd think he'd have been happy, but— just like so many other artists in history—it doesn't seem like he was at all. He'd climbed to the top of a mountain with *War and Peace*, but didn't like the view.

What else makes it hard to achieve our hopes and dreams?

Another limitation is your comfort zone. Your comfort zone is a fence. It's not until you push against it that you learn what sections of the fence are electric and where the fence can be leapt over with encouragement and help. I never guessed I'd be as scared as I was swimming with sharks, or feeding lions, or wrapping Didge the giant lizard around my neck. Beasts really do make me skittish. Considering I'm scared of hedgehogs, this shouldn't have come as a surprise. I'd expected to experience the sort of fear that makes things that little bit more fun, not for the beast boundary-fence to electrocute me. I didn't expect to be floating in a tank of sharks feeling so frightened I could hardly breathe.

When we're dealing with our own comfort levels, it's also impossible to tell whether we're being sensible or overly anxious. The extremes are easy. Jumping into a tiger cage wearing a dress made of steak is not sensible. On the other hand, living your life in fear of being abducted by aliens and subjected to invasive probing is not rational and points to more significant issues. For the things in between, it's harder to figure out. Like, how high is too high? How fast is too fast? Is doing the scary thing worthwhile and character-building, or is it okay to refuse because you're afraid? We carry our neuroses around like baggage, and all of our baggage is different.

The fences around our comfort zones are all in different places. One night at drinks someone asked me: 'If you had to lick a public toilet seat or walk into work naked, which would you choose?' The group was evenly split. A lively argument erupted about the relative merits of public shame versus hygiene. It wasn't resolved. The potential toilet-lickers couldn't understand the potential nudists, and vice versa. It seemed our comfort-zone fences were in very different places indeed.

There are times when our comfort-zone fences are a good thing. For the sake of decorum and good health, one really ought not to lick public toilet seats *or* go to work naked. Not wanting to do these things keeps us safe. This isn't always the case, though. Sometimes, our comfort-fences are barriers that stop us from being the best we could be.

During my year of new things, I became uncomfortably aware of my limitations and anxieties: heights; animals; feeling ugly; doing things alone; thinking I wasn't classy; worries about looking like a dick in public. One more thing for the list was public nudity. Early in the year, someone suggested going to a nudist colony for one of my new things.

'That sounds far too cold,' I said.

'You could go in summer,' they said. 'In the middle of summer, when it's really warm.'

I pretended to think it through.

'Nah,' I said. 'I get cold. I think it would still be too cold, even in the middle of summer.'

Someone else suggested a streak. A streak! Honestly! Did I *seem* like someone who would streak? There was one time I put 'Yay family steak night!' on Facebook. One friend said she'd thought I'd written 'Yay family streak night!' and sent me a menagerie of quizzical emojis. (I don't actually know what the collective noun is for emojis, but I think a menagerie sounds apt.) Regardless of what you call a group of emojis in one place, family steak night was the closest I had ever got to streaking, and I intended to keep it that way.

'I'm watering my plants that day,' I said. 'I think I'll be too busy.'

A few months later, someone else suggested naked poetry reading. Naked poetry! I didn't even know it was a thing before it was suggested as something I might like to do. You go to a public bar on a Friday night and read poetry dressed like you're in the Garden of Eden, but without the fig leaf. Every month has a different theme. The one I was invited to was entitled 'Crime and Punishment'.

Unlike the streaking and the nudist colony, I actually thought about it for a couple of weeks, weighing up the pros and cons. On one hand, *Crime and Punishment* is one of my favourite books in the world. On the other hand, given the context, I suspected it wouldn't be some sort of homage to Dostoevsky's masterpiece. But could I do it? I liked the idea of being cool with that sort of thing. *Yeah*, I thought. *I'm not harnessed by the shackles of conventional dress codes. I'm chill and fun and hip and body-confident. Naked poetry reading. Yeah!*

A friend then suggested being a life model, and—once

again—I pretended that I was cool with the idea in a futile attempt to convince myself that I actually was. I talked loudly about body confidence and the patriarchy and the favour I was doing Dahla by not being ashamed of my natural self. My friend went ahead with the life modelling. She sent me the contact details for the art school she'd modelled at. Of course I'd do it, I thought. It was just that there was always a good reason not to. It was on a Tuesday, and I had work. When I didn't have work during the time I was a stay-at-home mum, I was busy doing other things, like binge-watching television. Or it was too hot, or too cold, or too in-between. Or the weird stain on my bath required my full attention. My friend said she'd been told to do yoga poses. Yoga poses, while naked! I wish she hadn't told me that. Any chance I had of actually making life modelling one of my new things dissipated with any thoughts of naked downward dog. The email sat in my inbox for months before I admitted defeat and pressed delete.

And as for the naked poetry reading? I went to the cinema that evening instead. By myself. But I wasn't lonely. It was a nice evening, sitting in the dark, eating an ice cream that I hadn't dropped on the floor, unlike the night of 27 Rejections of Doom. I sat in the cinema and enjoyed being fully clothed. I felt happy. Like I said earlier in this book, there is a difference between loneliness and solitude, even though they look the same from the outside. Maybe all it takes is avoiding public displays of nudity to truly understand the difference.

So nudity was one comfort-fence I wasn't going to push against. I also backed out of getting a tattoo. My sister and I talked about getting one together, but, when it came to putting needle on flesh, she did it alone. Then, the hedgehog section of the fence. I was at the zoo once when a zookeeper was walking around with a hedgehog called Sonic. Sonic had been cleaned, and the keeper was letting children pat it. Jack stroked the evil beast's prickly back while I loitered in the shadows, trying to propel myself forward to touch it. I was too scared; in the shadows I remained. During my year of new things I approached the zoo and asked if Sonic was still there. Perhaps I could get close to him, and send my hedgehog phobia to Hades? But, alas, Sonic had died. Getting close to a hedgehog would not be one of my new things either.

I was comfortable with not doing those things. Not so with the one thing that haunted me—the 13-metre free-fall I'd been too scared to do when the Imp of the Scaredy-cat had got the better of me. The feeling of sheer terror had been lost in the sands of time, but the shame and regret I'd felt as I slunk away still lingered in the recesses of my mind. Falling would have been so easy. Why didn't I do it? I felt like I'd failed myself by being such a wuss. Plenty of my new things had taken me up high: Adrenalin Forest; bouldering; zip-lining; parasailing; a terrifyingly wobbly swing bridge on the overnight hike. Every single one of those things frightened me, but I did them anyway, and felt self-satisfied as a result. It was time to give the free-fall another go. But how to make myself go through with it? Same as last time, I couldn't have anyone there to take my photo, so couldn't rely on vanity and possible future bragging rights to carry me through. I wouldn't have anyone to egg me on. I was on my own.

What was holding me back? It wasn't money or faux dreaming or fear of failure or self-sabotage or not wanting to read poetry in my birthday suit. In this case, it was something much simpler: fear. Pure, unsexy, boring, relatable, run-of-the-mill fear.

The young man who handed me the wedgie-harness had some sage advice.

'You'll be freaked out as fuck, but once you're done, you'll be, like, fuck yeah,' he said.

When it was my turn, I shuffled to the end of the plank. All of a sudden, I had that feeling in the pit of my stomach that somehow linked to my feet and made me physically unable to move. Welcome back, Imp of the Scaredy-cat, my old nemesis. But this time was different. I was here. I couldn't fail twice. Before I could talk myself out of it, I closed my eyes, leaned backward and fell.

Fuck yeah?

Yeah, nah. I hated that free-fall with the white-hot passion of a thousand burning suns. When I landed, all I wanted to do was breathe deeply, kiss the dirt and cry, in no particular order.

I took off the wedgie-harness and looked back up at the platform I'd fallen off. It really *was* high. I smiled. I had finally had the courage to do that backward free-fall. And then the smugness seeped out of my pores.

The year of new things was over, and now I'd done the thing I'd regretted not doing the most.

Fuck yeah.

I did it.

In an odd way, I didn't feel finished. There are still so many other new things to do and my old purple notebook is still brimming with ideas. Seeing new places and experiencing new things is such an easy way to boost my confidence, give me something to look forward to and put a spring in my step. Doing things you've never done before wakes up your brain and makes you feel alive. I decided that, although I wouldn't continue doing new things with quite as much frequency or urgency, I would continue to try new things whenever it tickled my fancy. The world is an amazing place, and there are so many adventures to be had.

I hope my future script contains many such adventures. But, for the most part, I hope that my life is full of the nice little moments too. After my year of new things, I've decided that it's those moments that are the glue that hold contentment together.

I gave my harness back to Mr Fuck Yeah and went to meet Alan and the children. We'd arranged to meet at a cafe overlooking the forest where I'd done the free-fall. I'd promised the kids a bowl of hot chips, followed by ice cream in the sun.

And, in terms of the glue to hold my contentment together for the next year and beyond, that felt like a pretty good place to start.

# EPILOGUE

My year of new things was over when I got a letter. It was from my friend in Denmark, one of the people I'd written to months and months earlier for **new thing 17**. We hadn't lived in the same country for over twenty years, and had not seen each other for three. It was a long letter, the sort I hadn't been sent in at least a decade, possibly longer. I read it, then read it again, grin plastered to my face.

'Take care of yourself and thank you for continuing to make me part of your life,' she wrote. 'I love seeing your new things posts on Facebook. I really hope you write a book on your experiences.'

*I will,* I thought. I'll write about my year, and turn what I'd written thus far into some sort of narrative. This can be my new project. **New thing 54**: writing my story.

What an exciting prospect that would be.

# APPENDIX: THE COMPLETE LIST

1. Doing a confidence course through the forest treetops

2. Having a beauty-counter makeover

3. Having a manicure

4. Getting false eyelashes

5. Having a caricature drawn of myself

6. Wearing bright-red lipstick in public

7. Getting my 'colours' done

8. Going on acne medication

9. Going mountain biking

10. Trying dragon boating

11. Going bouldering

12. Entering a push-up competition

13. Shooting a bow and arrow

14. Doing a zip-line

15. Going in a helicopter

16. Detoxing from social media

17. Handwriting a letter to a friend or
family member every day for a week

18. Starting a virtual wine and Netflix group

19. Doing couple counselling

20. Swimming with sharks

**21.** Feeding lions

**22.** Doing a night tour of a wildlife sanctuary

**23.** Getting my tarot cards read

**24.** Riding a horse

**25.** Going to a planetarium

**26.** Making balloon animals

**27.** Going trick-or-treating

**28.** Going on the luge

**29.** Having a child-free holiday

**30.** Being a parent-helper

**31.** Keeping a gratitude journal

**32.** Going paddleboarding

**33.** Giving up alcohol for six months

**34.** Eating a vodka-infused doughnut

**35.** Learning to do pilates

**36.** Learning to play a song on the piano

**37.** Doing a watercolour painting class

**38.** Learning a hip-hop dance routine

**39.** Doing a cross-stitch

**40.** Going to a cooking masterclass

**41.** Riding a mechanical bull

**42.** Wrapping a giant lizard around my neck

**43.** Going go-karting

**44.** Doing an escape vault

**45.** Going to a political meet-the-candidates event and talking to every candidate

**46.** Going parasailing

**47.** Going to a music festival alone

**48.** Volunteering at a retirement village

**49.** Doing a DNA test

**50.** Doing an overnight hike

**51.** Entering a public dance competition

**52.** Performing stand-up comedy

## OTHER NEW THINGS (OR NEW THINGS 53 AND 54)

**53.** Doing a free-fall

**54.** Writing a non-fiction book

# NOTES

## 1: TWENTY-SEVEN REJECTIONS OF DOOM

1 Kieran Setiya, *Midlife: A philosophical guide*, Princeton: Princeton University Press, 2017, p. 23.
2 Sheryl Sandberg & Adam Grant, *Option B: Facing adversity, building resilience and finding joy*, London: Knopf, 2017.
3 Seth Stephens-Davidowitz, *Everybody Lies: Big data, new data and what the internet can tell us about who we really are*, New York: Dey Street Books, 2017, p. 31.
4 Mary Holm, *Rich Enough? A laid-back guide for every Kiwi*, Auckland: HarperCollins, 2018, p. 281.
5 Adam Hart-Davis, *Pavlov's Dog: and 49 other experiments that revolutionised psychology*, London: Modern Books, 2018, pp. 125–27.

## 2: THE THIRD UGLIEST

1 Andy Boyle, *Adulthood for Beginners: All the Life Secrets Nobody Bothered to Tell You*, New York: TarcherPerigee, 2017, pp. 192–94.
2 Stephens-Davidowitz, p. 125.

3  Stephens-Davidowitz, p. 136.

4  S. Ramrakha et. al, 'Cumulative Mental Health Consequences of Acne: 23-year follow-up in a general population birth cohort study', British Journal of Dermotology, <onlinelibrary.wiley.com/doi/full/10.1111/bjd.13786>, 2015, accessed 26 March 2020.

5  Ramrakha et al.

6  David McRaney, *You Are Not So Smart: Why you have too many friends on Facebook, why your memory is mostly fiction, and 46 other ways you're deluding yourself*, New York: Avery, 2012, pp. 162–65.

7  Roxane Gay, *Hunger: a memoir of (my) body*, London: Corsair, 2017, p. 136.

8  Marleen Gorris (dir.), *Within the Whirlwind*, 2009. I also love Taryn Brumfitt's quote: 'Your body is not an ornament, it's the vehicle to your dreams'. Brumfitt's Body Image Movement as captured in the 2016 film *Embrace* is a must-watch for anyone interested in finding out more about this issue.

9  This also links to the concept of 'ego depletion', as described in Daniel Kahneman, *Thinking, Fast and Slow*, London: Penguin, 2012, pp. 41–44, and 'losing the cool system' as described in Walter Mischel, *The Marshmallow Test: Understanding self-control and how to master it*, London: Transworld, 2014, pp. 49–50.

# 3: COMMUNICATION, OLD AND NEW

1  Tim Smith, 'The Demise of the Landline', *Canstar Blue* <canstarblue.co.nz/phone-internet/bundled-communication-plans/demise-of-the-landline>, 2015, accessed 29 March 2020.

2  Guy P. Harrison, *Think Before You Like: social media's effect on*

*the brain and the tools you need to navigate your newsfeed*, New York: Prometheus, 2017, p. 18.

3  Harrison, p. 136.

4  Harrison, pp. 134–35.

5  Harrison, p. 151.

6  Stephens-Davidowitz, pp 112–27.

7  Although it is apparently linked to a belief in soulmates. For more on this see Robert P. Burriss, 'Why Do Some People Vanish from Relationships?, *Psychology Today*, <psychologytoday.com/blog/attraction-evolved/201804/ghosting-why-do-people-end-relationships-disappearing?collection=1114539>, 2018, accessed 29 March 2020.

8  For more on phubbing, see Susan Krauss Whitbourne, 'There's a New Way to Make Someone Feel Inferior', *Psychology Today*, <psychologytoday.com/blog/fulfillment-any-age/201804/theres-new-way-make-someone-feel-inferior>, 2017.

9  Aaron Smith, 'What People Like and Dislike About Facebook, *Pew Research Center*, <pewresearch.org/fact-tank/2014/02/03/6-new-facts-about-facebook>, 2014.

10  For more information about the theory since dubbed 'Dunbar's number', see Malcom Gladwell, *The Tipping Point*, London: Abacus, 2000, pp. 177–81. See also McRaney, pp. 146–50 and Harrison, p. 28.

11  This isn't necessarily meant in a derogatory way as 'Is my husband gay?' is a common search. For more, see Seth Stephens-Davidowitz, pp. 160–61.

12  'Why Your Cellphone Has More Germs than a Toilet Seat', The University of Arizona College of Agriculture and Life Sciences, <cals.arizona.edu/news/why-your-cellphone-has-more-germs-toilet>, 2012.

13  Susan Krauss Whitbourne, 'Is Facebook Making You Depressed?', *Psychology Today*, <psychologytoday.com/

blog/fulfillment-any-age/201710/is-facebook-making-you-depressed>, 2017, accessed 29 March 2020.

14 Stephens-Davidowitz, p. 99.

15 Graham C. L. Davey, 'Social Media, Loneliness and Anxiety in Young People', *Psychology Today*, <psychologytoday.com/blog/why-we-worry/201612/social-media-loneliness-and-anxiety-in-young-people>, 2016.

16 For more on the Internet Addiction Test and the Bergen Facebook Addiction Scale see Harrison, pp. 156–58.

17 I write about this in more detail here: <thenaturalparentmagazine.com/social-media-feels-like-know-actually-know-less>.

18 Extracts of this section are also published here: <thespinoff.co.nz/society/04-12-2017/social-media-a-broken-friendship-and-mental-health>.

19 Mattha Busby, 'Cambridge Considers Typed Exams as Handwriting Worsens', <theguardian.com/education/2017/sep/09/cambridge-considers-typed-exams-as-handwriting-worsens>, 2017, accessed 29 March 2020.

# 4: LOVE, MARRIAGE, HORSE, NO CARRIAGE

1   Greg Behrendt and Liz Tuccillo, *He's Just Not That Into You*, London: HarperCollins, 2005, p. 111.

2   Amir Levine and Rachel S. F. Heller, *Attached: The new science of adult attachment and how it can help you find—and keep—love*, New York: TarcherPerigee, 2010, p. 28.

3   Susan Heitler, 'Love: 13 reasons why it may not lead to marriage', *Psychology Today*, <psychologytoday.com/blog/resolution-not-conflict/201410/love-13-reasons-why-it-may-not-lead-marriage>, 2014, accessed 29 March 2020.

4   Levine and Heller, p. 268.

5  Rachel Clayton, 'Divorce Rate Declining as Kiwis Marry Later in Life', Stuff, <stuff.co.nz/life-style/love-sex/88235010/divorce-rate-declining-as-kiwis-marry-later-in-life>, 11 January 2017.

6  For more information on how dopamine works, see <psychologytoday.com/basics/dopamine>.

7  See Shauna H. Springer, 'Falling in Love is Like Smoking Crack Cocaine', *Psychology Today*, <psychologytoday.com/blog/the-joint-adventures-well-educated-couples/201208/falling-in-love-is-smoking-crack-cocaine>, 2012, accessed 29 March 2020.

8  As quoted in Daniel Klein, *Every Time I Find The Meaning of Life, They Change It: wisdom of the great philosophers on how to live*, Melbourne: Penguin, 2015, p. 71.

9  Louis de Bernières, *Captain Corelli's Mandolin*, New York: Vintage, 1995, p. 281.

10 As quoted in Klein, pp. 73–74.

11 Aaron Ben-Zeév, 'What Do Singles Really Want?', *Psychology Today*, <psychologytoday.com/blog/in-the-name-love/201802/what-do-singles-really-want>, 2018, accessed 29 March 2020.

12 Holm, p. 287.

13 For more about instant gratification, see Mischel.

14 Keane, *Tear Up This Town*, 2016.

15 Shirley P. Glass, *Not Just Friends': Rebuilding trust and recovering your sanity after infidelity*, New York: Atria Books, 2003, p. 22.

16 For more on this see Brené Brown, *Rising Strong: How the ability to reset transforms the way we live*, London: Vermillion, 2015.

17 Hart-Davis, pp. 125–26.

18 Glass, p. 23.

19 McRaney, pp. 82–86.

20 For more on this see Ben Goldacre, *Bad Science*, London: Fourth Estate, 2009, pp. 242–55.

21 Sarah Bartlett, *The Tarot Bible: The definitive guide to the cards and*

*spreads*, London: Godsfield, 2006, p. 15.

22 Bill Bryson, *A Short History of Nearly Everything*, London: Doubleday, 2003, p. 573.

## 5: PART-TIME MUM

1 For more on this see Brené Brown, *Daring Greatly: How the courage to be vulnerable transforms the way we live, love, parent, and lead*, New York: Avery, 2012. In particular Chapter Seven, 'Wholehearted Parenting: Daring to be the adults we want our children to be', pp. 214–43.

2 Bartlett.

## 6: A FEW QUIET DRINKS AND A BIT OF BANTER

1 Stephens-Davidowitz, p. 19.

2 'Who's Drinking and How Much', *Wellplace.nz*, <wellplace. nz/facts-and-information/alcohol/drinking-in-new-zealand>.

3 For the test, see <alcohol.org.nz/help-advice/is-your-drinking-ok/is-your-drinking-okay-test/the-test>.

4 Russell Brand, *Recovery: Freedom from our addictions*, London: Picador, 2017, p. 43.

5 Annie Grace, *This Naked Mind: Control alcohol, find freedom, discover happiness and change your life*, New York: Avery, 2018, pp. 6–7.

6 For more on peer pressure and drinking, see Grace, p. 51.

## 7: BEING A CLASSY LADY

1 For more about this see Brown, *Daring Greatly*.

# 8: LONELINESS, THE STEALTH NINJA OF FEELINGS

1 For more on the difference between loneliness and solitude, see Klein, pp. 68–69.

2 Johann Hari, *Lost Connections: Uncovering the real causes of depression—and the unexpected solutions*, New York: Bloomsbury, 2018, pp. 74–76.

3 Julianne Holt-Lunstad's study as quoted in 'These Three Moves Will Help You Stop Feeling Lonely', *Psychology Today*, <psychologytoday.com/blog/brainstorm/201712/these-three-moves-will-help-you-stop-feeling-lonely>, 2017, accessed 29 March 2020.

4 This is one of the reasons the UK has established a Minister for Loneliness. See 'Minister for Loneliness Appointed to Continue Jo Cox's Work, BBC, <bbc.com/news/uk-42708507>, 2018.

5 Mischel, pp. 160–61.

6 As quoted in Klein, p. 30.

7 Ellen Hendriksen, *How To be Yourself: Quiet your inner critic and rise above social anxiety*, New York: St Martin's Press, 2018, p. 14.

8 Brené Brown, *Braving the Wilderness: The quest for true belonging and the courage to stand alone*, London, Random House, 2017, p. 55. Brown also writes extensively about the link between loneliness and shame, writing: 'we all feel shame around being lonely—as if feeling lonely means there's something wrong with us.'

9 As described in Mischel, p. 132.

10 For more information about this see Alex Williams, 'Why Is It Hard to Make Friends Over 30?', *The New York Times*, <nytimes.com/2012/07/15/fashion/the-challenge-of-making-friends-as-an-adult.html>, 2012, accessed 29 March 2020. See also my article detailing my thoughts in more depth: *Natural Parent Magazine*, 'Is It Harder to Make Friends When You're

Older?', <thenaturalparentmagazine.com/harder-make-friends-youre-older>, 2017, accessed 29 March 2020.

11 Dr Seuss, *Green Eggs and Ham*, London: HarperCollins, 2003.

12 The theory of transactional analysis is one worth reading up on. It has helped me understand why some conversations with certain people go badly and why some interpersonal relationships don't work well. For more information see <ericberne.com/transactional-analysis>.

13 This is also called the fundamental attribution error, which is detailed in McRaney, pp. 264–74.

14 Gwendolyn Seidman, *Psychology Today*, 'Do Facebook "Likes" Affect Psychological Wellbeing?', <psychologytoday.com/blog/close-encounters/201610/do-facebook-likes-affect-psychological-well-being>, 2016, accessed 29 March 2020.

15 Seidman.

16 For more about the spotlight effect see McRaney, pp. 162–65.

## 9: A CIRCULAR LINE TO DOING NOT MUCH

1 Edith Eger, *The Choice: Even in hell hope can flower*, London: Ebury, 2017, p. 205.

2 I've deliberately stayed out of the debate on the role of brain chemistry as a cause of depression here, but for more information on this I recommend Hari, *Lost Connections*.

3 Richie Poulton, Terrie E. Moffitt and Phil A. Silva, 'The Dunedin Multidisciplinary Health and Development Study: Overview of the first 40 years, with an eye to the future', *Social Psychiatry and Psychiatric Epidemiology*, 2015, vol. 50, no. 5, p. 687.

4 Hari, p. 11.

5 Hari, p. 13.

6 Hari, pp. 147–48.

# 10: THE BEST JOKE IN THE ROOM

1   As quoted in Elan Gale, *You're Not That Great (But Neither is Anyone Else)*, New York: Hachette, 2017, p. 51.

2   This is listed between 'When the person in line ahead of you at Starbucks can't make up her mind and you are legit in a hurry' and 'When other women pee on the seat'. Sarah Knight, *The Life-Changing Magic of Not Giving a F\*\*k*, New York: Little Brown and Company, 2015, p. 98.

3   Jon Olb and Madeleine Parry (dir.), *Hannah Gadsby: Nanette*, 2018.

# 11: NEW THING 53

1   This is referenced in Kahneman, p. 63.

2   As quoted in Setiya, p. 38.

# BIBLIOGRAPHY

*ʍɪɪˈˈˈʍɪˈˈˈʍʍˈʍˈˈʍ*

## ARTICLES

Ben-Zeév, Aaron, 'What Do Singles Really Want?', *Psychology Today*, <psychologytoday.com/blog/in-the-name-love/201802/what-do-singles-really-want>, 2018, accessed 29 March 2020

Burriss, Robert P., 'Why Do Some People Vanish from Relationships?, *Psychology Today*, <psychologytoday.com/blog/attraction-evolved/201804/ghosting-why-do-people-end-relationships-disappearing?collection=1114539>, 2018, accessed 29 March 2020

Busby, Mattha, 'Cambridge Considers Typed Exams as Handwriting Worsens', *The Guardian*, <theguardian.com/education/2017/sep/09/cambridge-considers-typed-exams-as-handwriting-worsens>, 9 September 2017, accessed 29 March 2020

Clayton, Rachel, 'Divorce Rate Declining as Kiwis Marry Later in Life', *Stuff*, <stuff.co.nz/life-style/love-sex/88235010/divorce-rate-declining-as-kiwis-marry-later-

in-life>, 11 January 2017, accessed 7 August 2020

Davey, Graham C. L., 'Social Media, Loneliness, and Anxiety in Young People', *Psychology Today*, <psychologytoday.com/ blog/why-we-worry/201612/social-media-loneliness-and-anxiety-in-young-people>, 2016, accessed 7 August 2020

Heitler, Susan, 'Love: 13 reasons why it may not lead to marriage', *Psychology Today*, <psychologytoday.com/blog/ resolution-not-conflict/201410/love-13-reasons-why-it-may-not-lead-marriage>, 2014, accessed 29 March 2020

Keenan, Lauren, 'Is It Harder to Make Friends When You're Older?', *Natural Parent Magazine*, <thenaturalparentmagazine.com/harder-make-friends-youre-older>, 2017, accessed 29 March 2020

——, 'Social Media: It feels like we know more, but do we actually know less?', *Natural Parent Magazine*, <thenaturalparentmagazine.com/social-media-feels-like-know-actually-know-less>, 2017, accessed 7 August 2020

Krauss Whitbourne, Susan, 'Is Facebook Making You Depressed?', *Psychology Today*, <psychologytoday.com/ blog/fulfillment-any-age/201710/is-facebook-making-you-depressed>, 2017, accessed 29 March 2020

—— 'There's a New Way to Make Someone Feel Inferior', *Psychology Today*, <psychologytoday.com/blog/fulfillment-any-age/201804/theres-new-way-make-someone-feel-inferior>, 2018, accessed 7 August 2020

'Minister for Loneliness Appointed to Continue Jo Cox's Work', *BBC*, <bbc.com/news/uk-42708507>, 2018, accessed 7 August 2020

Poulton, Richie, Terrie E. Moffitt and Phil A. Silva, 'The Dunedin Multidisciplinary Health and Development Study: Overview of the first 40 years, with an eye to the future', *Social Psychiatry and Psychiatric Epidemiology*, 2015, vol. 50, no. 5, pp. 679–93

Ramrakha, S., et al., 'Cumulative Mental Health Consequences of Acne: 23-year follow-up in a general population birth cohort study', *British Journal of Dermatology*, <onlinelibrary.wiley.com/doi/full/10.1111/bjd.13786>, 2015, accessed 26 March 2020

Seidman, Gwendolyn, 'Do Facebook "Likes" Affect Psychological Well-Being?', *Psychology Today*, <psychologytoday.com/blog/close-encounters/201610/do-facebook-likes-affect-psychological-well-being>, 2016, accessed 29 March 2020

Smith, Aaron, 'What People Like and Dislike About Facebook', *Pew Research Center*, <pewresearch.org/fact-tank/2014/02/03/6-new-facts-about-facebook>, 2014, accessed 7 August 2020

Smith, Tim, 'The Demise of the Landline', *Canstar Blue*, <canstarblue.co.nz/phone-internet/bundled-communication-plans/demise-of-the-landline>, 2015, accessed 29 March 2020

Springer, Shauna H., 'Falling in Love Is Like Smoking Crack Cocaine', *Psychology Today*, <psychologytoday.com/blog/the-joint-adventures-well-educated-couples/201208/falling-in-love-is-smoking-crack-cocaine>, 2012, accessed 29 March 2020

'These Three Moves Will Help You Stop Feeling Lonely',
*Psychology Today*, <psychologytoday.com/blog/
brainstorm/201712/these-three-moves-will-help-you-stop-
feeling-lonely>, 2017, accessed 29 March 2020

'Who's Drinking and How Much', *Wellplace.nz*, <wellplace.
nz/facts-and-information/alcohol/drinking-in-new-
zealand>, accessed 7 August 2020

'Why Your Cellphone Has More Germs Than a Toilet Seat',
*The University of Arizona College of Agriculture and Life Sciences*,
<cals.arizona.edu/news/why-your-cellphone-has-more-
germs-toilet>, 2012, accessed 7 August 2020

Williams, Alex, 'Why Is It Hard to Make Friends Over 30?',
*The New York Times*, <nytimes.com/2012/07/15/fashion/
the-challenge-of-making-friends-as-an-adult.html>, 13 July
2012, accessed 29 March 2020

## BOOKS: NON-FICTION

Bartlett, Sarah, *The Tarot Bible: The definitive guide to the cards and
spreads*, vol. 7, London: Godsfield, 2006

Behrendt, Greg, and Liz Tuccillo, *He's Just Not That Into
You: The no-excuses truth to understanding guys*, London:
HarperCollins, 2005

Boyle, Andy, *Adulthood for Beginners: All the life secrets nobody
bothered to tell you*, New York: TarcherPerigee, 2017

Brand, Russell, *Recovery: Freedom from our addictions*, London:
Picador, 2017

Brown, Brené, *Braving the Wilderness: The quest for true belonging and the courage to stand alone*, London: Random House, 2017

───── *Daring Greatly: How the courage to be vulnerable transforms the way we live, love, parent, and lead*, New York: Avery, 2012

───── *Rising Strong: How the ability to reset transforms the way we live, love, parent, and lead*, London: Vermillion, 2015

Bryson, Bill, *A Short History of Nearly Everything*, London: Doubleday, 2003

Eger, Edith, *The Choice: Even in hell hope can flower*, London: Ebury, 2017

Gale, Elan, *You're Not That Great (But neither is anyone else)*, New York: Hachette, 2017

Gay, Roxane, *Hunger: A memoir of (my) body*, London: Corsair, 2017

Gladwell, Malcom, *The Tipping Point: How little things can make a big difference*, London: Abacus, 2000

Glass, Shirley P., *Not 'Just Friends': Rebuilding trust and recovering your sanity after infidelity*, New York: Atria Books, 2003

Goldacre, Ben, *Bad Science*, London: Fourth Estate, 2009

Grace, Annie, *This Naked Mind: Control alcohol, find freedom, discover happiness & change your life*, New York: Avery, 2018

Hari, Johann, *Lost Connections: Uncovering the real causes of depression—and the unexpected solutions*, New York: Bloomsbury, 2018

Harrison, Guy P., *Think Before You Like: Social media's effect on the brain and the tools you need to navigate your newsfeed*, New York: Prometheus, 2017

Hart-Davis, Adam, *Pavlov's Dog: and 49 other experiments that revolutionised psychology*, London: Modern Books, 2018

Hendriksen, Ellen, *How to Be Yourself: Quiet your inner critic and rise above social anxiety*, New York: St Martin's Press, 2018

Holm, Mary, *Rich Enough? A laid-back guide for every Kiwi*, Auckland: HarperCollins, 2018

Kahneman, Daniel, *Thinking, Fast and Slow*, London: Penguin, 2012

Klein, Daniel, *Every Time I Find the Meaning of Life, They Change It: Wisdom of the great philosophers on how to live*, Melbourne: Penguin, 2015

Knight, Sarah, *The Life Changing Magic of Not Giving a F\*\*k*, New York: Little Brown and Company, 2015

Levine, Amir and Rachel S. F. Heller, *Attached: The new science of adult attachment and how it can help you find—and keep—love*, New York: TarcherPerigee, 2010

McRaney, David, *You Are Not So Smart: Why you have too many friends on Facebook, why your memory is mostly fiction, and 46 other ways you're deluding yourself*, New York: Avery, 2012

Mischel, Walter, *The Marshmallow Test: Understanding self-control and how to master it*, London: Transworld, 2014

Sandberg, Sheryl & Adam Grant, *Option B: Facing adversity, building resilience and finding joy*, London: Knopf, 2017

Setiya, Kieran, *Midlife: A philosophical guide*, Princeton: Princeton University Press, 2017

Stephens-Davidowitz, Seth, *Everybody Lies: Big data, new data, and what the internet can tell us about who we really are*, New York: Dey Street Books, 2017